ARTISTS

INSPIRING STORIES OF THEIR LIVES AND WORKS

Written by Susie Hodge

Illustrated by Jessamy Hawke

Author Susie Hodge
Illustrator Jessamy Hawke
Historical consultant Dr Stephen Haddelsey

Editor Kat Teece
Designer Brandie Tully-Scott

Additional editorial Olivia Stanford, Marie Greenwood, Kieran Jones
Additional design Bettina Myklebust Stovne, Holly Price, Sif Nørskov, Rob Perry
US Senior Editor Shannon Beatty
US Editor Mindy Fichter
Publishing Coordinator Issy Walsh
Senior Picture Researcher Rituraj Singh
Managing Editor Jonathan Melmoth
Managing Art Editor Diane Peyton Jones
Senior Production Editor Nikoleta Parasaki
Senior Production Controller Leanne Burke
Publishing Director Sarah Larter

First American Edition, 2022
Published in the United States by DK Publishing
1450 Broadway, Suite 801, New York, NY 10018

Copyright 2022 Dorling Kindersley Limited
DK, a Division of Penguin Random House LLC
22 23 24 25 26 10 9 8 7 6 5 4 3 2 1
001-326563-Jul/2022

Published in Great Britain by Dorling Kindersley Limited.

A catalog record for this book is available from the Library of Congress.
ISBN: 978-0-7440-5667-9

DK books are available at special discounts when purchased in bulk for sales promotions, premiums, fund-raising, or educational use. For details, contact: DK Publishing Special Markets, 1450 Broadway, Suite 801, New York, NY 10018 SpecialSales@dk.com

Printed and bound in China

For the curious
www.dk.com

MIX
Paper | Supporting responsible forestry
FSC™ C018179

This book was made with Forest Stewardship Council ™ certified paper—one small step in DK's commitment to a sustainable future.

For more information go to www.dk.com/our-green-pledge

CONTENTS

Before 1800

1800 to 1900

After 1900

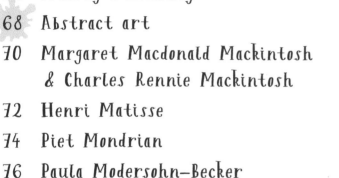

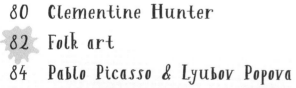

FOREWORD
by Susie Hodge

People have been making art for tens of thousands of years, since long before paper and pencils even existed. The first artists scratched patterns and pictures on rocks, or smeared crushed stones or blood on to cave walls. Since that time, different civilizations have produced their own art—and we can tell a lot about what life was like for them by the artworks they made. Most societies have developed their own styles, traditions, and rules of art. So, if you learn what to look for, you can often figure out roughly when and where certain works of art were made—like an art detective.

Individual artists make art for many different purposes. They might want to show religious or spiritual ideas, or what they believe to be right and wrong behavior. They might want to show others what particular people, animals, or objects look like or mean to them, or to record important events. Some artists simply want to make the world more beautiful, or to inspire reactions from the people looking at their art. Artists have even made art because they believed it would perform magic, or summon or please gods.

In this book, you will meet many artists who worked at different times and in different places, and who each created outstanding art. Many of the artists were poor, and did not make much money from their art. Others became rich from it. They came from all sorts of backgrounds. Some from poor families, some from rich. Some did well at school, others struggled. Some were unknown during their lives and became famous after they died, some were celebrated while they lived.

However, nearly all artists have one thing in common: They make art because they love it. I hope the artists in this book will inspire you to seek out art, and to make your own. Because art and artists enrich our world.

Susie Hodge

BEFORE 1800

Early humans used natural materials (including their own blood) to create paintings, prints, carvings, and sculptures. As time passed, new art materials, such as oil paints, were invented, artists developed their skills, and artistic movements began to spread. All the artists in this chapter were born before the year 1800.

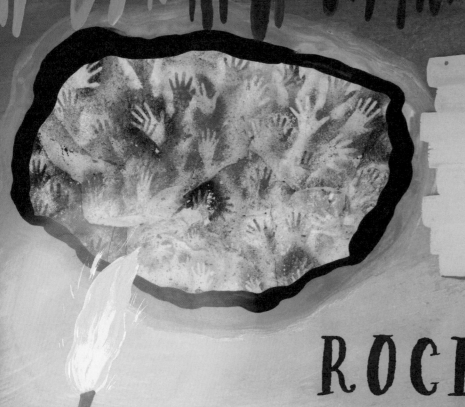

Handprints

Some early artists placed their hands on cave walls and blew paint over them through hollow bird bones. When they took their hands away, the shapes of their hands were left unpainted on the wall.

ROCK ART

Thousands of years ago, before paper or canvases were invented, people began making art on rocks or deep inside caves. Some daubed soft clay onto cave walls, then scratched images into it. Others used stone tools to scratch pictures onto the surface, and some painted with crushed minerals.

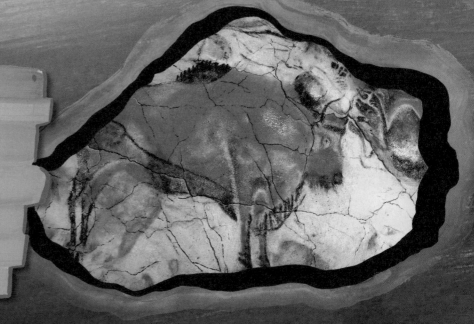

Animals

It is not known why prehistoric artists painted animals. However, some people think that they believed painting the animals they hunted would "capture" them, which would make it easier to catch the animals in real life.

Activities
"Prehistoric" means before writing was invented, so cave art is one of the few clues we have about how people lived long ago. Some cave art shows humans acting out everyday activities, such as hunting, though it was much more likely to show animals on their own.

Extinct animals
Some rock and cave art features animals that are now extinct. They include a cave lion (shown above), giant prehistoric elephants called mastodons, prehistoric horses, and giant sloths.

Different methods
Cave artists made paint by mixing crushed natural materials, such as earth, chalk, colored stones, and berries, with spit or animal fat. They applied the paint with twigs, moss, animal hair, or bones, or blew it through hollowed-out bones.

Religion
Prehistoric cave art created deep inside caves, where no one lived, may have been made as part of religious rituals. The creators of the art are thought to have been important religious people believed to have magical powers, called shamans.

The full title of **Thutmose** was "The King's Favorite and Master of Works." The sculptor worked for the Pharaoh Akhenaten and Queen Nefertiti in around 1300 BCE. Thutmose and his family lived in a house next to his large workshop. He created many sculptures, especially busts of the pharaoh's family, and was an important member of the royal court.

Most ancient Egyptian art was stylized—which meant it was made to look a certain way rather than be a lifelike copy of what it was depicting. The Egyptians believed that their gods could understand images more easily if they were simplified. However, Thutmose's art was lifelike and natural-looking.

Thutmose lived in the city of Akhetaten, newly built as the Pharaoh Akhenaten's capital. It was abandoned soon after the Pharaoh's death, but the ruins survive to this day.

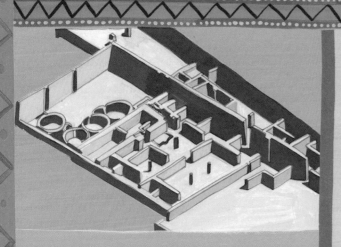

Archaeologists discovered Thutmose's workshop attached to his house in Akhetaten. Inside were around fifty sculptures that Thutmose had left behind, including one of Pharaoh Akhenaten.

Sculpting the queen

In Thutmose's workshop was a bust—a statue showing only the head and shoulders —of Queen Nefertiti, who the ancient Egyptians saw as a living goddess. One eye is rock crystal—the other is lost.

THUTMOSE

Egyptian sculptor • c.1300s BCE

Iron oxide

To paint his sculptures, Thutmose made brushes out of bundled twigs, palm leaves, or knotted rope.

Making paint

Minerals, found in rocks, were crushed to make some Egyptian paints. These minerals included iron oxide, limestone, azurite, and lapis lazuli.

Life after death

An ancient Egyptian word for sculptor means "he who keeps alive." This was because the ancient Egyptians believed that if they created a long-lasting statue of someone, then that person would exist forever—even after death. Many people wanted statues made of themselves for this reason. Thutmose and his assistants were kept busy, carving statues of the rich and famous out of hard stone. His workshop was like a factory.

Thutmose used limestone to carve busts of the royal family. He smoothed out the rough surface with stucco—a plaster made from the rock gypsum, which was ground to a powder and made into a paste with water.

Not much else is known about Thutmose's life, and many of his artworks are lost. Most of them were probably used to decorate the homes of their subjects, or perhaps were placed in tombs, which may have been looted in the thousands of years since he was alive.

However, Thutmose's workshop was discovered in 1912, with a precious bust of Nefertiti left intact on the floor. Possibly made for his assistants to copy and learn from, or simply an unwanted artwork, this bust, and others in the workshop, show the talent of Thutmose—the pharaoh's sculptor.

TIMARETE
Ancient Greek painter • 5th century BCE

Most of the artists written about by the ancient Greeks were men, who were seen as more important than women. The first of the six female painters recorded was Timarete.

She appears by three other names in the history books—Thamyris, Tamaris, and Thamar—and there are only a few things known about her life. She was the daughter of a painter who lived and worked in the busy Greek city of Athens, named Micon the Younger, so it is likely that she was born there. She is famous for her painting of the goddess Artemis that was on display at Ephesus, an ancient Greek city that has long since been turned to ruins. The artwork of Artemis was lost, too— along with many others we will probably never know about.

The philosopher and Greek historian Pliny the Elder, wrote about Timarete and Irene in his book Natural History. *He lived in the first century CE, around 100 years after Irene, and 500 years after Timarete.*

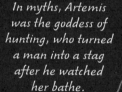

In myths, Artemis was the goddess of hunting, who turned a man into a stag after he watched her bathe.

Ancient Greek artists aimed for perfection. As with more recent centuries, different types of art came in and out of fashion. During Timarete's time, artists made lively art, which showed exciting scenes and movement.

Going against the grain

Pliny wrote that Timarete "scorned the duties of women and practiced her father's art." This meant that she did not work in the home— cooking, cleaning, and sewing—as women were expected to do.

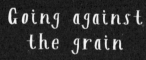

IRENE

Ancient Greek painter • 1st century BCE

Like Timarete, Irene was given different **names** by historians, since the correct version became muddled over time. Also called Yrenes and Eirene, she was written about by several Greek historians—and then again more than 1,000 years later by the 14th-century Italian author Giovanni Boccaccio.

Irene was taught to paint by her father, the artist Cratinus, in Athens. She famously painted a picture of a maiden (young woman). Historians think this figure may have been someone who was looked after by the Greek goddess Demeter, who was seen as a mother figure. Irene was also inspired by entertainers. Giovanni Boccaccio wrote that she painted a juggler and at least two famous performers of her time—a dancer and a gladiator.

Irene's paints were probably encaustic (wax-based) or tempera, made from a sticky material such as egg and powdered color.

Gladiators were ancient Roman fighters who battled each other to entertain audiences. Their popularity spread to Greece, where some became famous.

Dancing was often a part of religious ceremonies, performed with instruments including lyres, lutes, and kitharas. It could be energetic or slow, depending on the event.

Juggling was a popular form of entertainment in ancient Greece. Most jugglers were women.

13

The lost wax method

In this bronze-sculpting method probably used by Myron, a clay model is created. Wax is molded around it and coated in more clay, leaving a hole. This is heated so the wax melts and runs out of the hole, then hot, liquid bronze is poured in. The bronze cools and takes the clay mold's shape.

MYRON
Ancient Greek sculptor
5th century BCE

Statues from the ancient Greek world still survive today—more than 2,000 years later. However, many more of them have been broken or lost over time. Myron was one of the artists who made these sculptures.

Myron created statues for temples, where the Greek gods were worshipped, for tombs, and to stand as monuments, which celebrated important people as well as the gods. He used materials such as marble, bronze, wood, and gleaming gold.

Many artists, writers, philosophers (thinkers and early scientists), and teachers lived in Athens.

Myron's cow sculpture that stood in the marketplace was so lifelike that other people—and animals—thought it was real!

Myron's Discus Thrower captures the moment an athlete is about to throw a discus.

Most of Myron's time was spent in the ancient Greek city-state of Athens—a bustling place built around the Acropolis, or "high town." His lifelike sculptures were mostly made of bronze, and showed gods and heroes from Greek myths. However, Myron became especially known for his athletes in action, and animals. The other details of Myron's life have been lost over time.

PHIDIAS
Ancient Greek sculptor
c.488—431 BCE

Like his fellow sculptor Myron, Phidias lived and worked in Athens. As well as a sculptor, he was a painter and architect, which means someone that designs buildings. His earliest works included a huge bronze statue of the goddess Athena, which towered over the city. Phidias also designed and supervised the building of the Parthenon, a grand marble temple dedicated to the same goddess. He is thought to have used an idea called "the Golden Ratio," which is a way of using proportions and measurements to achieve perfect balance.

Phidias's huge, wooden statue of Zeus was covered in ivory (elephant tusk), and had gold and precious stone details. It reached the ceiling of the temple in which it sat.

Phidias's colossal statue of Zeus, the king of the gods, took him twelve years to make, and became one of the Seven Wonders of the World. But while he was celebrated as a younger artist, he was later accused by his enemies of stealing costly materials from his statues of Athena and Zeus. Luckily, he was found innocent, and people continued to celebrate his artwork.

Only later Roman copies of Phidias's sculptures exist today. They were probably painted in bright colors that have worn off.

Athena
At 30 ft (9 m) high, Phidias's bronze sculpture Athena Promachos was massive. It celebrated a Greek victory over the Persians. Promachos means "leading warrior," and Athena was dressed in armor, a spear in her right hand.

ANCIENT SCULPTURE

Artists belonging to ancient civilizations across the world skilfully carved and molded detailed sculptures. They used materials with different colors and textures, including rocks such as basalt, limestone, and marble, and metals such as bronze. Some sculptures have survived, so we can see which subjects inspired artists thousands of years ago.

Sekhmet

The ancient Egyptians often made sculptures of their gods. Each god was linked to a part of life, such as love, and they had special features, such as animal heads. This statue shows Sekhmet, the goddess of healing and war, who had a lion's head.

Charioteer of Delphi

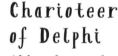

Although many bronze sculptures were made in ancient Greece, most of these haven't survived, because they were melted down to make weapons and other objects. One of the best-known surviving bronze statues is this winner of a chariot race.

Colossal head

This huge marble head is one of the few remaining parts of a colossal statue of Constantine, an ancient Roman emperor. The figure is estimated to have been 40 ft (12 m) tall—around the height of a three-story building! It stood in Rome, the capital of the Roman Empire.

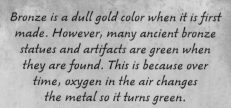

Bronze is a dull gold color when it is first made. However, many ancient bronze statues and artifacts are green when they are found. This is because over time, oxygen in the air changes the metal so it turns green.

The ram in the thicket

This is one of two identical statues made in Mesopotamia, in what is now Iraq, between 2600 and 2400 BCE. Different, colorful materials were used by the artist, including the precious blue stone lapis lazuli, copper, and gold. The figurines may have been created to encourage crops to grow—or simply for decoration.

Mother goddess

The writings of the ancient Indus Valley civilization are in a language we can't yet read, so we can only guess what they wrote about. They left behind small clay figures, which are thought to have been used for religious purposes. This one may show a mother goddess, perhaps made to bring luck to people who wanted a child.

Terra-cotta is made from clay, which is molded into the desired form and then fired in an oven until it hardens.

Jade

In ancient China, jade, known as *yu*, was a popular material for sculpture. It was thought to show purity, beauty, or even immortality, and artists carved jade sculptures to honor important people, such as leaders. The jade in these precious sculptures had to be carved delicately, with soft tools.

The rough outer layer of jade has to be polished away to reveal the green color the stone is known for.

The old woman

From Pliny's writing, we know that Iaia painted a large portrait of an old woman on a wooden panel. Like many paintings from ancient Rome, this probably rotted or crumbled away.

Iaia found plenty of work in the bustling city of Rome. At the time, Rome was full of gleaming marble temples and palaces, and over a million people lived there. It was the largest city in the world.

Long before selfies were invented, Iaia was said to be the first artist to make a self-portrait. She was born in Cyzicus, an ancient Greek town in what is now Turkey, and grew up to be a famous painter and ivory (elephant tusk) carver.

Not much is known about Iaia's life, except that she left Cyzicus for Rome at some point, where she produced most of her work. Other female artists of that time trained with their fathers or older brothers, but it is not known whether Iaia did this. She was written about by an ancient author called Pliny the Elder, who mentioned her groundbreaking self-portrait. He also wrote that most of her paintings were of women.

IAIA
Ancient Roman painter and carver • c.116—27 BCE

Ivory was a popular material for engraving, or carving, designs into. This required a lot of skill and patience. Today, people realize that taking ivory from elephants is cruel.

Roman art

Most ancient Roman artwork that remains today are either paintings on stone walls, such as the one above, mosaics, or statues made of marble or bronze. None of Iaia's paintings have survived, as far as we know.

Determined to make it

Iaia painted on wood, linen cloth, and marble, using two main types of paint—tempera and encaustic. Tempera is made of powdered pigment (color) mixed with water and a binder, such as starch. Encaustic is a method of painting using hot wax and oils mixed with pigments.

Unusually for the period, Iaia never married, which meant that she did not have to spend time looking after a family like most other women. Instead, she could concentrate on being an artist. She would have had to be determined to become successful in a male-dominated world.

The most famous painters of the time were two male artists called Sopolis and Dionysius. However, it is thought that Iaia earned more money than them by working faster.

ARANIKO
Nepalese painter, sculptor, and architect
1245—1306

From a young age, Araniko was talented at art. He was said to have been better at calligraphy (artistic ways of writing) than his teachers. Araniko became an expert in painting and model-making, too—and designed impressive structures such as the White Stupa, which still stands today.

When Araniko was sixteen, the the emperor who established China's Yuan dynasty, Kublai Khan, asked the king of Nepal to send artists and craftsmen to the mountain city of Lhasa. Kublai Khan wanted them to create statues and a golden stupa (temple). The king of Nepal summoned eighty artisans and watched them work. He chose the best, Araniko, and put him in charge of the group. The resulting work was so good that it caught the eye of the powerful emperor.

The White Stupa
After the stupa in Lhasa was built, Kublai Khan asked Araniko to build another one, in China's capital city, Dadu (now Beijing). This white stupa took ten years to build.

The Emperor of China made Araniko famous, and gave him a lot of important work. He was Kublai Khan, grandson of the mighty Genghis Khan, and he ruled over China and the Mongol Empire.

Silk

Araniko painted on silk, a material woven from thread spun by silkworms. Each worm makes a long, silk strand to wrap around itself many times as a cocoon. Inside, it changes into a moth.

Silk moth cocoon

Silk moth caterpillar

Great honors

Kublai Khan decided to further test Araniko's skills. He asked Araniko to repair a bronze statue, a task so complex that it would take two years. Araniko did the job absolutely perfectly. He was never again out of work.

Araniko created many ornate statues, and monasteries, temples, and shrines for different religions—including Buddhism, Confucianism, and Daoism. He also painted portraits of the emperor and other important people. Kublai Khan made him "the Master of all Classes of Artisans" and gave him the honor of a grand silver plate to wear, with a tiger on it. After he died, Araniko was given the important titles of Ming Hoi and the Duke of Liang.

Adult silk moth

As well as his beautiful buildings, Araniko painted portraits of people at the Chinese court using colorful ink on silk. This is a noble lady of the imperial court.

21

PAINTING PEOPLE

People have been painting themselves and others for thousands of years. Paintings of people are called portraits and are often made to show what a person is like in real life— both how the person looks and what their personality is like. Some portraits have been made to show other things as well, such as how important a person is to others.

Painting the dead

When a rich ancient Egyptian died, their image was usually painted on their sarcophagus (a case for their body). Originally, these pictures were stylized, or not meant to be exact copies. Later, when the Roman Empire took control of Egypt, realistic portraits such as this one were placed on top of wooden coffins instead.

Not quite lifelike

In Europe between the 400s and 1400s, portraits of people from the Bible did not look realistic. Baby Jesus often looked like a small man, because he was thought to have been born as a "homunculus"—Latin for "little man."

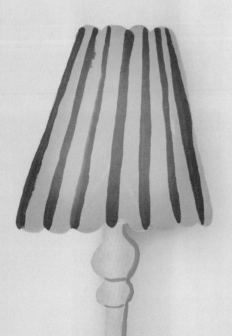

Becoming real

In the centuries before the 1600s, people in European portraits were often made to look "perfect." Later, artists became more interested in trying to capture each subject's personality. This portrait of an unknown sitter by Jan Vermeer uses clever brushstrokes to make the girl look real.

Self-portraits

Self-portraits are portraits made by artists of themselves. This might show how they see themselves, for example what their talents are. In this portrait by Sofonisba Anguissola (c.1532–1625), the artist shows herself painting. Other artists may choose themselves as subjects simply because they are there to copy.

Some artists have had mirrors placed in galleries, suggesting that the viewer is the work of art!

Abstract portraits

In the early 1900s, some artists started depicting people in abstract (un-lifelike) ways. They often used unnatural colors and simplified shapes to build the image. The artists were trying to show things about the person in the portrait that weren't visible, such as their kindness or intelligence.

Photographing people

Photographs are now a favorite way of capturing people's portraits, and many portrait photographers aim to capture a person's personality, too. They might do this with props, lighting, makeup, poses, expressions, clothing, or composition—which is how the image is arranged.

Power in paint

Portraits of kings and queens are often seen in national galleries. Monarchs were among the few who could afford to pay artists to paint them in the past. Today, portraits often celebrate elected leaders, such as the former US president Barack Obama (shown here in a painting by Kehinde Wiley).

SHEN ZHOU
Chinese poet and painter
1427—1509

Throughout history, various writers and artists like Shen have rejected wealth and powerful jobs and instead focused on becoming great artists and poets.

The Wu, or Wu School, was a group of artists who worked during the Ming Dynasty of imperial China. Wu paintings were created by scholarly artists and they usually have writing on them, describing the picture with the date and reason it was painted. The Wu School was started by Shen Zhou.

Shen grew up in a rich family, near the busy city of Suzhou, China. After his father died, Shen looked after his mother, but rather than working for the government, as was expected of him, he spent his life reading, writing poetry, and painting.

Blossoming ink
Shen used long, fine, and detailed brushstrokes in his earlier works. Later, he painted with broad, thick, and energetic strokes.

New painting style

The word "literati" was used to describe certain people of Shen's time, who were well-educated. The literati included writers or poets. Their work was "literary" in style and subject. This means it was thoughtful, and often focused on expressing feelings.

Shen was part of the literati, and he also learned history and the traditional Chinese styles of painting and calligraphy (writing letters artistically). The ideas he learned as part of the literati can be seen in his art. He also invented his own flowing style of painting, which started a new art trend. In particular, Shen became famous for his artworks of landscapes and flowers.

Chinese landscape artists were expected to paint scenes realistically, but Shen did not just copy what he saw. Instead, he painted as he felt, to express his inner feelings.

Many educated people at the time were skilled poets and artists. The poets wrote poems on their paintings, or on paintings that others had painted.

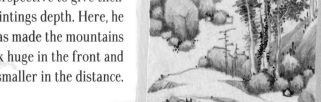

Perspective

Shen and other Chinese landscape artists used perspective to give their paintings depth. Here, he has made the mountains look huge in the front and smaller in the distance.

ALBRECHT DÜRER

German painter and printmaker
1471—1528

The son of a goldsmith, Albrecht Dürer grew up to be known as the "Prince of German artists." He was inspired by Italian Renaissance artists to create detailed drawings, engravings, and natural-looking paintings. He carefully copied what he saw in real life in lifelike drawings. After he left school in his home city of Nuremberg, Albrecht trained as a goldsmith with his father. But by the time he was fifteen, his talent for drawing was too good to ignore. He became an apprentice to a local artist who was well-known at the time, named Michael Wolgemut. In his early twenties, Albrecht visited Italy and from then on his art was transformed.

Woodcut engravings were one of the earliest printing techniques, made by pressing ink onto paper using a carved block of wood. Albrecht's engravings were detailed, with fine lines.

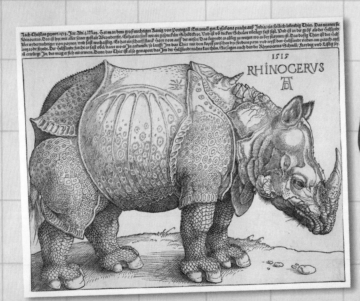

Hand studies

Albrecht spent a lot of time trying to draw things as accurately as possible. Some of his most famous drawings are of hands. Detailed and lifelike, he may have created them simply to show off his skills.

Bringing Italy to Germany

When Albrecht returned to Nuremberg, he began working differently from most other artists there. While they focused on creating natural, ordinary-looking art, Albrecht was influenced by the grander Italian Renaissance style, in which every person and place was meant to look 'idealistic,' or beautiful and perfect. Albrecht soon became famous for his work and made friends with many of the most important artists in Europe. He became a member of Nuremberg's Great Council, which discussed issues related to the city. He was even asked to create art for the Holy Roman Emperor.

Albrecht wanted to make convincing images of the real world, so he used grids and drawing frames which split up the image into smaller squares to copy.

Albrecht earned a lot of money from his art. Some of his most important works were portraits of wealthy people.

Lifelike images

As well as using grids, Albrecht came up with his own ways to copy what he saw. One of his methods was to use string to measure angles of objects he was drawing.

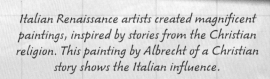

Italian Renaissance artists created magnificent paintings, inspired by stories from the Christian religion. This painting by Albrecht of a Christian story shows the Italian influence.

27

Art above your head

It took four years to paint the vast Sistine Chapel ceiling with more than three hundred figures. This artwork is a buon fresco, which is a painting made on wet plaster so that the color dries into it.

When **Pope Julius II** (the head of the Catholic Church) first asked Michelangelo to paint a ceiling in his palace in the Vatican City, Michelangelo said no since he preferred sculpting to painting. But the Pope convinced him, and today millions of visitors a year go to marvel at this work.

Born in Florence, Italy, Michelangelo became an apprentice to the painter Domenico Ghirlandaio at the age of thirteen. He went on to study sculpture at a school set up by the powerful Medici family. As an adult, Michelangelo became known for incredibly lifelike sculptures, such as *David*, and was able to find work in cities across Italy, including Florence and Rome. Despite preferring sculpture, his overhead painting in the Vatican's Sistine Chapel was one of Michelangelo's best achievements. A poet and an architect as well, he was nicknamed by the Italian people "Il Divino," or "The Divine One."

Michelangelo's first works included the marble sculpture Pietà, showing Jesus and his mother Mary from Christian Bible stories. He carved cold, hard marble to look like warm, soft flesh.

MICHELANGELO
Italian painter and sculptor • 1475—1564

The Raphael libraries

Elsewhere in the Pope's grand home, Raphael was asked to paint large frescoes on plain walls. He was only in his mid-twenties at the time, in 1508.

Raphael was born in Urbino in central Italy, which was an important center for art at the time. His father was a painter and poet working for the local Duke, and Raphael learned how to paint from him.

After his father died when Raphael was eleven, he moved to Perugia, where he worked with a well-known painter, Pietro Perugino. Raphael developed his own style of painting and moved to Florence when he was twenty-one. There, he saw art made by Leonardo da Vinci and Michelangelo, the most famous artists of the time, who inspired him to paint beautiful figures. In 1514, Raphael was made the Pope's chief architect and designed several important buildings. He became extremely popular, and when he died from an illness in Rome on his thirty-seventh birthday, hundreds of mourners followed Raphael's coffin to its resting place—the ancient Roman Pantheon.

Raphael designed ten tapestries for Pope Leo X, to hang in the Sistine Chapel. After he created the designs, they were sent to Brussels to be woven.

RAPHAEL
Italian painter • 1483—1520

Chiaroscuro

Using tonal contrasts (different shades of color) makes paintings look 3D. Some Renaissance artists led the way for artists to paint with dramatically strong light and dark tones. This technique is called "chiaroscuro" from the Italian words *chiaro* meaning "light" and *scuro* meaning "dark."

A painting of Mary Magdalene, a Christian saint, by Titian.

Perspective

Renaissance artists figured out several ways to make paintings look 3D (not flat). They painted distant objects smaller than those that are closer, as they would appear in real life, as can be seen in this ancient Greek-inspired painting by Raphael. Showing depth and distance like this is called perspective.

THE RENAISSANCE

Sfumato

First used during the Renaissance, sfumato (Italian for "smoky"), is a painting technique that involves making shadows look especially soft and blurry. Leonardo da Vinci used this technique skilfully, in paintings such as the *Mona Lisa* (shown here).

New ideas in European art and science from the 1300s to the 1600s led people to call this period "The Renaissance," which means "rebirth" in French. Unlike previous generations, Renaissance artists were inspired by the stories, art, and buildings of ancient Greece and Rome. They also came up with new painting techniques.

Artists revived ideas from the second century of painting "putti" (from the Latin word "putus" for boy), which were chubby little boys with wings.

New paints

Oil paint, made of pigment mixed with a light-colored oil, was first used during the Renaissance. This type of paint is easy to blend. In the oil painting below by Giovanni Bellini, showing the Christian figures of Mary and Jesus, the colors blend from one shade to another.

Myths and legends

Greek and Roman myths became popular subjects of Renaissance art. One myth tells of the Roman goddess Venus being born from sea-foam—the painting above, by Sandro Botticelli, shows her arriving at the shore.

Sculpture

Renaissance artists created statues that closely copied the human form. These were inspired by ancient Greek and Roman sculptures, which were often shown in active poses and had lifelike muscles. Michelangelo's *David* (shown here) is a famous example.

Look up! Artists were paid to paint detailed murals across the walls and ceilings of important buildings, such as palaces. This room in the Vatican took several years to complete, and was based on drawings by Raphael.

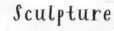

SHIN SAIMDANG
Korean painter and calligrapher
1504—1551

Encouraged to paint from the age of seven by her father and grandfather, Shin Saimdang soon branched out to other types of art. Saimdang lived at a time when men were seen as more important than women, but she became celebrated as a painter, writer, calligrapher, and poet.

Despite Saimdang's fame, many things are unknown about her. Even her name may have been a made-up pen name, used to sign pieces of writing. However, we do know she was raised in a village in Kangwon Province, Korea. There, she grew up in the house of her grandparents, with her parents and four sisters. She was given the same good quality education as boys, and her family supported her artistic skills.

Saimdang's grandparents' home still stands today. Saimdang gave birth to her famous son, Yulgok, there. She said she dreamed of dragons before he was born.

Calligraphy

The art of beautiful handwriting, as seen on this artwork by Saimdang, was developed more than 5,000 years ago. Calligraphers use a special brush to make it.

Painting

Saimdang began a type of painting called *Chochungdo*. It showed landscapes and garden scenes featuring insects, plants, and animals, painted onto screens for decorating rooms.

32

Carer and creator

As she grew up, Saimdang developed her skills in calligraphy, which is the art of beautiful writing, and embroidery, the art of forming decorative designs with needlework. Saimdang married at 19, though she continued to live with her parents so that she could care for them. She had seven children, but she still found time for her art even though she was busy looking after so many people. She also read the texts of a belief system called Confucianism, which tells people how to live their life well.

Saimdang's work began to be admired by many—especially her bright, lifelike paintings. These were said to have been so realistic that chickens pecked holes in one of her screens as they tried to eat the painted insects. Sadly, because she was a woman, Saimdang was not allowed to sign her artwork. On top of the 40 that are confirmed, there could be many more works of art that no one knows are hers.

Saimdang was the first woman to appear on a Korean banknote.

Saimdang's son Yulgok, also known as Yi I, became a famous scholar. Like Saimdang, he is featured on a Korean banknote.

Embroidery

Saimdang embroidered flowers, such as those in the artwork above, and other images. Embroidery was a popular art form in Korea, and was used on clothes, cushions, tablecloths, and pojagi (cloths for wrapping and carrying items).

33

ARTEMISIA GENTILESCHI
Italian painter • 1593—1656

Paintings such as this by Caravaggio (1571–1610) inspired many artists of Artemisia's day. His characters showed strong emotions, and Artemisia is famoed for showing her female figures' emotions.

By the time she was nineteen, Artemisia Gentileschi's artist father, Orazio, wrote in a letter that his daughter had no equal as a painter. She later became one of the era's most sought-after female artists.

Born and raised in Rome, Italy, Artemisia was taught to paint by her father. In Rome, women at the time were largely expected to stay at home. Without studios, female artists could mostly only paint flowers, or self-portraits. But Artemisia began to paint figures, probably based on the family's servants.

Baroque art

Religious paintings became especially dramatic in the 1600s, such as this painting by Artemisia of a biblical scene. This style was later called Baroque art, from the Portuguese for "misshapen pearl" as an insult after it was no longer fashionable.

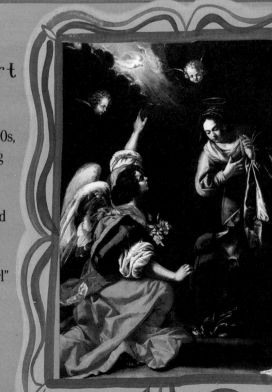

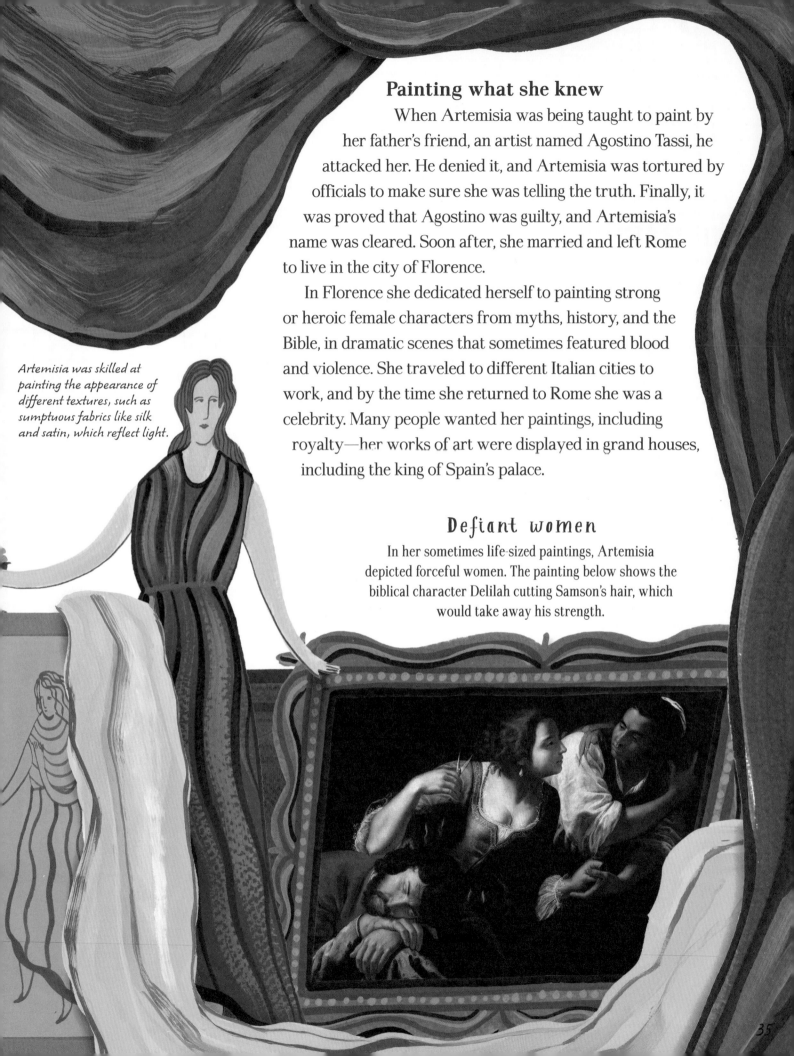

Painting what she knew

When Artemisia was being taught to paint by her father's friend, an artist named Agostino Tassi, he attacked her. He denied it, and Artemisia was tortured by officials to make sure she was telling the truth. Finally, it was proved that Agostino was guilty, and Artemisia's name was cleared. Soon after, she married and left Rome to live in the city of Florence.

In Florence she dedicated herself to painting strong or heroic female characters from myths, history, and the Bible, in dramatic scenes that sometimes featured blood and violence. She traveled to different Italian cities to work, and by the time she returned to Rome she was a celebrity. Many people wanted her paintings, including royalty—her works of art were displayed in grand houses, including the king of Spain's palace.

Artemisia was skilled at painting the appearance of different textures, such as sumptuous fabrics like silk and satin, which reflect light.

Defiant women

In her sometimes life-sized paintings, Artemisia depicted forceful women. The painting below shows the biblical character Delilah cutting Samson's hair, which would take away his strength.

REMBRANDT VAN RIJN

Dutch painter • 1606—1669

There was no shortage of people paying for portraits in Rembrandt van Rijn's Amsterdam—then the wealthiest city of Europe. Rembrandt grew up in the capital city of what is now the Netherlands and left university to become apprenticed to two different artists. At seventeen, he opened his own studio with another artist, and by his mid-twenties, he was the leading portrait painter to the richest families in the city.

For the next twenty years, he worked constantly, painting portraits and earning a lot of money. Many rich people's sons came to him as pupils and he taught them to copy his style. He became even wealthier when he married Saskia van Uylenburgh, who came from a well-off family.

Etching

Rembrandt's favored printmaking technique involves smoothing wax onto a copper or zinc plate. Next, a design is scratched into the wax. The design is dipped in acid, which cuts into the plate beneath the scratched lines, but does not affect the parts protected by wax. Ink is then added, so it sinks into the etched lines and can be transferred onto paper.

The etched design is covered in ink.

Paper is pressed against the inked copper plate to transfer the image.

Rembrandt became known for his skillful painting of light and darkness. His figures are often shown in realistic-looking candlelight.

Some of Rembrandt's paintings show ancient myths, often featuring beautiful scenery. This painting shows the Cretan princess Europa being kidnapped by the Greek god Zeus, in the form of a bull.

Riches to rags

Rembrandt and Saskia bought a magnificent house in the most expensive part of town. He began collecting works of art, antiques, clothes, jewelry, and opulent props to use in paintings.

Unlike most artists of his time, Rembrandt did not go to Italy to study the art of the Italian masters, but he knew about them through prints and the ideas other artists brought back. He started using the Italian style of looser brush marks and chiaroscuro.

Rembrandt's later life was less fortunate. Saskia died young, and his art fell out of fashion. No longer able to sell his paintings, he instead had to sell almost everything he owned.

"Practice what you know, and it will help to make clear what now you do not know."

Self-portraits

Rembrandt drew and painted himself throughout his life, showing how he aged. In some paintings, he showed himself in furs, gold chains, or other grand costumes.

KATSUSHIKA HOKUSAI

Japanese woodblock artist
1760—1849

One of the most famous Japanese artists ever, Katsushika Hokusai even has his own emoji! The emoji shows one of his woodblock prints—*Under the Wave off Kanagawa*. However, Hokusai did much more than just print art. He began as a painter, and went on to create drawings and illustrated books. Hokusai grew up in Edo, one of the largest cities in the world at the time. As an adult, he found a studio in the city to work in. It was common for Japanese artists to use different names if they changed their style of art—and Hokusai tried out so many styles that he changed his name more than thirty times!

Hokusai made several books containing pictures showing Mount Fuji, which is a sacred place for Japanese people. His pictures show Mount Fuji from different viewpoints, in different seasons.

In front of an audience at a festival in Edo, using brooms and buckets of ink, Hokusai painted a huge 600 ft (180 m)-long portrait, of Daruma, a Buddhist priest.

Hokusai won a painting competition by making a sweep of blue paint, then letting a chicken run over it after he had dipped its feet in red paint. He said the footprints were "maple leaves on the Tatsuta River."

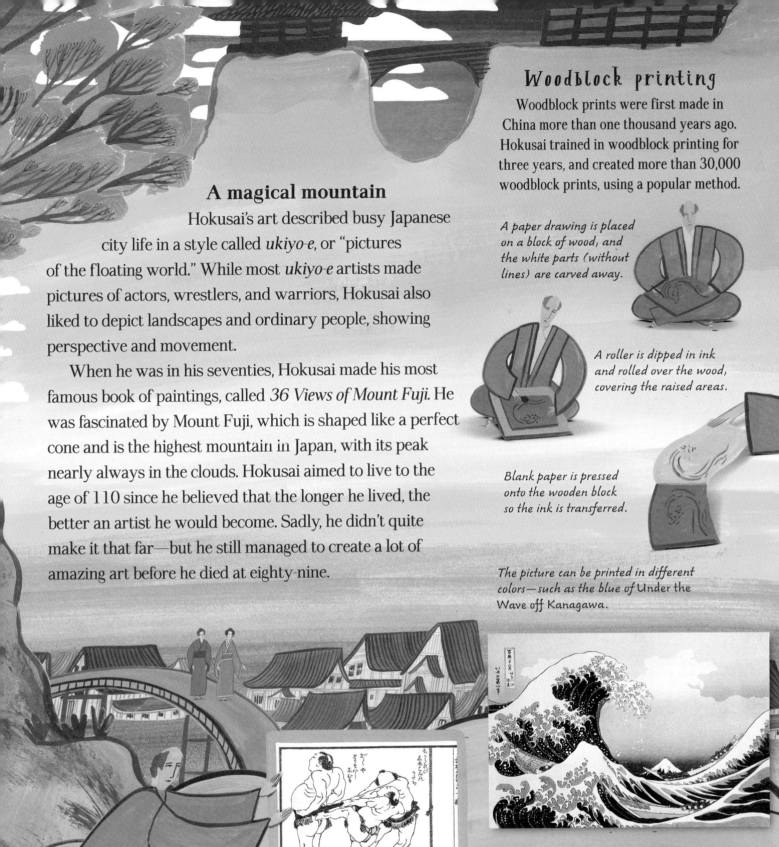

A magical mountain

Hokusai's art described busy Japanese city life in a style called *ukiyo-e*, or "pictures of the floating world." While most *ukiyo-e* artists made pictures of actors, wrestlers, and warriors, Hokusai also liked to depict landscapes and ordinary people, showing perspective and movement.

When he was in his seventies, Hokusai made his most famous book of paintings, called *36 Views of Mount Fuji*. He was fascinated by Mount Fuji, which is shaped like a perfect cone and is the highest mountain in Japan, with its peak nearly always in the clouds. Hokusai aimed to live to the age of 110 since he believed that the longer he lived, the better an artist he would become. Sadly, he didn't quite make it that far—but he still managed to create a lot of amazing art before he died at eighty-nine.

Woodblock printing

Woodblock prints were first made in China more than one thousand years ago. Hokusai trained in woodblock printing for three years, and created more than 30,000 woodblock prints, using a popular method.

A paper drawing is placed on a block of wood, and the white parts (without lines) are carved away.

A roller is dipped in ink and rolled over the wood, covering the raised areas.

Blank paper is pressed onto the wooden block so the ink is transferred.

The picture can be printed in different colors—such as the blue of Under the Wave off Kanagawa.

Hokusai made fifteen drawing manuals that he called "Hokusai manga," showing figures such as wrestlers. They were the first manga, which is what Japanese comic books are called.

BOOM!

CARTOONS

The word "cartoon" originally described drawings that were used as plans for paintings or tapestries. Nowadays, cartoons are usually drawn in the artist's own special way, with specific features, such as thick outlines or bright colors. A modern cartoon often tells a story, and can be animated or still.

Storytelling
Cartoons are a good way of telling stories because artists can make characters look however they want—even if the characters are imaginary creatures. They can also make them do things that aren't possible in real life.

Caricatures
In caricatures, individuals are often shown with exaggerated features, to try to make viewers laugh. This image depicts two eighteenth-century leaders—the UK's William Pitt (on the left) and France's Napoleon (on the right). One is skinny and tall, and the other is particularly short.

Stylish art

The same subject drawn by several cartoonists can look completely different, because all artists have their own styles. For example, they might exaggerate certain features of an animal or human, such as the eyes.

Manga

This form of Japanese cartoon often features characters with large eyes that are used to show emotion. Symbols, such as lightning bolts, are also used to indicate characters' feelings. Animated manga is called "anime."

Comic strips

A comic strip features several still scenes in a row that tell a story. When many strips are combined, they can be made into a comic book. Some of the most famous comics are based on the adventures of superheroes, such as Superman or Wonder Woman.

ADÉLAÏDE LABILLE-GUIARD

French painter • 1749—1803

The French royals of Adélaïde Labille-Guiard's time spent money on grand clothes, parties, food, and grand palaces. They also paid for paintings from the most skilled artists, such as Adélaïde.

Adélaïde grew up comfortably in Paris, France. Unlike many girls at the time, who were not educated, she was lucky enough to study painting with several artists, including a miniaturist and pastel artist, and she attended art school. From early on in her career, Adélaïde's art was considered good enough to be shown regularly at an important exhibition held once a year in Paris, called the Salon.

Adélaïde was passionate about female education, and famously painted herself teaching female students.

Miniatures

These tiny paintings were popular in Adélaïde's time. They were often portraits made for loved ones, who would carry them in their pockets or wear them on chains.

In 1795, Adélaïde became the first female artist to be given a teaching studio in the Louvre Museum, Paris, along with an allowance of money.

Leading the charge

Adélaïde was the first woman to become a member of the highly respected French Royal Academy (an organization of artists). She tried to improve the chances of other women, too, by teaching aspiring female painters and asking the Royal Academy to accept more women. She also believed the French government should make sure girls from poor families were educated.

Adélaïde's studio was always busy with students, who watched in awe as she produced skilful miniatures, pastels, and oil paintings. Despite the opposition of many men, Adélaïde was asked to paint portraits of members of the royal family. However, during the French Revolution, many of her paintings were destroyed by the royals' enemies.

Fit for royalty

Only the best portraitists are chosen to paint royalty, and several aunts of King Louis XVI asked Adélaïde to create theirs. This painting of the king's aunt, Marie Louise Élisabeth, was requested by Marie's sisters.

The French Revolution began in 1789. Under the king's rule, many people in France were extremely poor, while the royals and wealthy landowners lived in luxury. The people protested and then violently rebelled, killing the king and taking control of the government.

43

1800 to 1900

Until 1800, **most famous artists** aimed to show the physical world around them. Then, after the first photograph was taken in 1826, some art started to show things that photos could not, such as feelings. Many new art movements developed in Europe, with with people creating art that was different from the art that had been made before.

ROSA BONHEUR
French painter • 1822—1899

Animaliers

Rosa was an animalier. This group of artists were mainly from the nineteenth century, and became known for painting or sculpting realistic-looking animals.

Lions are not usually found in the gardens of French houses. But eccentric Rosa Bonheur so enjoyed painting their impressive manes and athletic bodies that she brought some to live on the grounds of her château! She painted and sculpted many more animals, too, and became world-famous for her art.

At their home in Bordeaux, France, Rosa's artist father taught all his four children to draw, paint, and sculpt. He also brought animals into his studio for them to draw. Rosa's mother saw her passion for animals and used it to help Rosa learn to read and write—she asked her to choose and draw a different animal for each letter of the alphabet.

Rosa kept stags, wild boars, a gazelle, lions, and other animals on the sprawling grounds of her house.

The horse fair
One of Rosa's most famous
works was her wall-sized
painting *The Horse Fair*.
It showed a market held
in Paris, and captured the
strong bodies of the horses.

Animal art

As she grew older, Rosa eagerly sought out more animals to draw and
paint, and visited animal markets around Paris. In 1841, two of her
artworks were displayed at the Paris Salon, an important exhibition
held each year. It was the start of a successful career.

During her mission to draw animals as accurately as possible,
Rosa spent many hours studying animal anatomy (the body)
at the National Veterinary Institute in Paris. Her hard
work paid off, and her paintings won many
awards. She also became the first woman to
receive the French Legion of Honour.
Through her success, she bought a big
house in the countryside, where she
kept many beloved animals.

*In the 1800s, women in
pants was rare—it was
even illegal for them to
wear pants in Paris.
Rosa gained the police's
permission to wear pants
to dirty animal markets,
and hardly ever wore
skirts again.*

HARRIET POWERS

African American folk artist
1837—1910

Harriet was born into slavery, which means she was made to do grueling physical work without pay on a large farm, called a plantation. Harriet's plantation probably grew cotton, which means she spent many long hours picking this fluffy substance from plants in the fields.

When she was 18, Harriet married another enslaved person, Armstead, and the couple soon welcomed the first of their nine children. Harriet started putting her hands to more creative use by learning to make quilts. Far from just useful items, Harriet's quilts featured striking appliqué (sewn-on fabric shapes). She was inspired to create scenes from stories—both local tales and stories from the Bible, which she learned about at church.

Plantations in the USA grew different crops, such as cotton, coffee, and sugar. Most plantations had communities of around fifty enslaved people.

Bible Quilt

Each of the eleven panels (squares) on this quilt tells a different Bible story in a colorful and symbolic way. Harriet made the quilt out of three hundred pieces of fabric, stitching by hand and with her sewing machine.

Pictorial Quilt

This quilt has fifteen panels showing scenes from the Bible, African symbols, and stories about the weather and stars. The Bible scenes include a story about a man named Jonah being swallowed by a whale (panel 6), and the first humans—Adam and Eve (panel 4).

This panel shows a famously cold day in 1895—with icicles hanging from a mule's mouth!

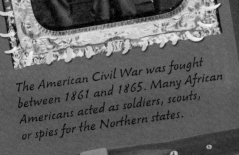

The American Civil War was fought between 1861 and 1865. Many African Americans acted as soldiers, scouts, or spies for the Northern states.

Sew good

In 1861, civil war broke out between the Southern states of the USA, that wanted to keep people as slaves, and the Northern states, which didn't. The Northern states won, and Harriet and her family were free.

Harriet and Armstead acquired a small farm of their own, where Harriet continued creating quilts. In 1886, she decided to exhibit her Bible Quilt for others to admire at the Athens Cotton Fair. There, another artist, Jennie, asked if she could buy the quilt, but Harriet wanted to keep it. Four years later, Harriet and Armstead needed more money, so she agreed to sell the quilt to Jennie. She described each scene so that Jennie could make notes, and through her careful descriptions, today we know exactly what each panel shows.

The word "appliqué" comes from the French word for "to apply." The technique involves sewing a smaller piece of fabric onto a larger piece to create a design.

AUGUSTE RODIN

French sculptor • 1840—1917

One of the most famous sculptors of all time became an artist through his love of drawing. Born in Paris, France, Auguste Rodin struggled at school due to his poor eyesight, but he loved drawing.

As a teenager, he studied drawing and painting, but was not accepted at an important French art school, the École des Beaux-Arts. Instead, he took a job making decorative stonework. After Auguste's sister died, a priest advised him that becoming a sculptor would help him cope with his grief. Auguste traveled to Italy, where he was stunned by the work of Michelangelo. Back in Paris, Auguste created lifelike sculptures, which people loved because they expressed emotions.

The Thinker

Balancing his chin on one hand, *The Thinker* is one of Auguste's most famous works. It represents someone using his imagination. It may be a self-portrait of Auguste.

Auguste liked to show how his sculptures were made. He left tool marks and fingerprints on them, or exhibited clay models that most sculptors would have had copied into marble or bronze.

CAMILLE CLAUDEL
French sculptor • 1864—1943

At just twelve years old, a French sculptor named Camille Claudel was creating work good enough to catch the eye of a professional sculptor. The sculptor told her father that she should train at college, and her journey to becoming a great artist began.

She studied at the Académie Colarossi, and went on to share a studio with three other female sculptors. Her sculpted figures were lifelike, graceful, and expressed emotions.

The great sculptor, Auguste Rodin, gave advice to the sculptors at this studio, and Camille became his assistant. The two fell in love—and this love inspired Camille to create romantic sculptures of couples. After Auguste refused to leave his girlfriend for her, Camille became so upset that eventually her family sent her to live in a hospital for people with mental illnesses.

Old age

Camille was interested in showing the effects of age on the body. The old lady in this sculpture is Clotho, one of three mythical Greek characters called Fates, who controlled what happened to humans.

Claudel became Auguste's muse, which means she posed for him. He made several sculptures of her, such as the one above.

51

EDMONIA LEWIS
American sculptor
1844—1907

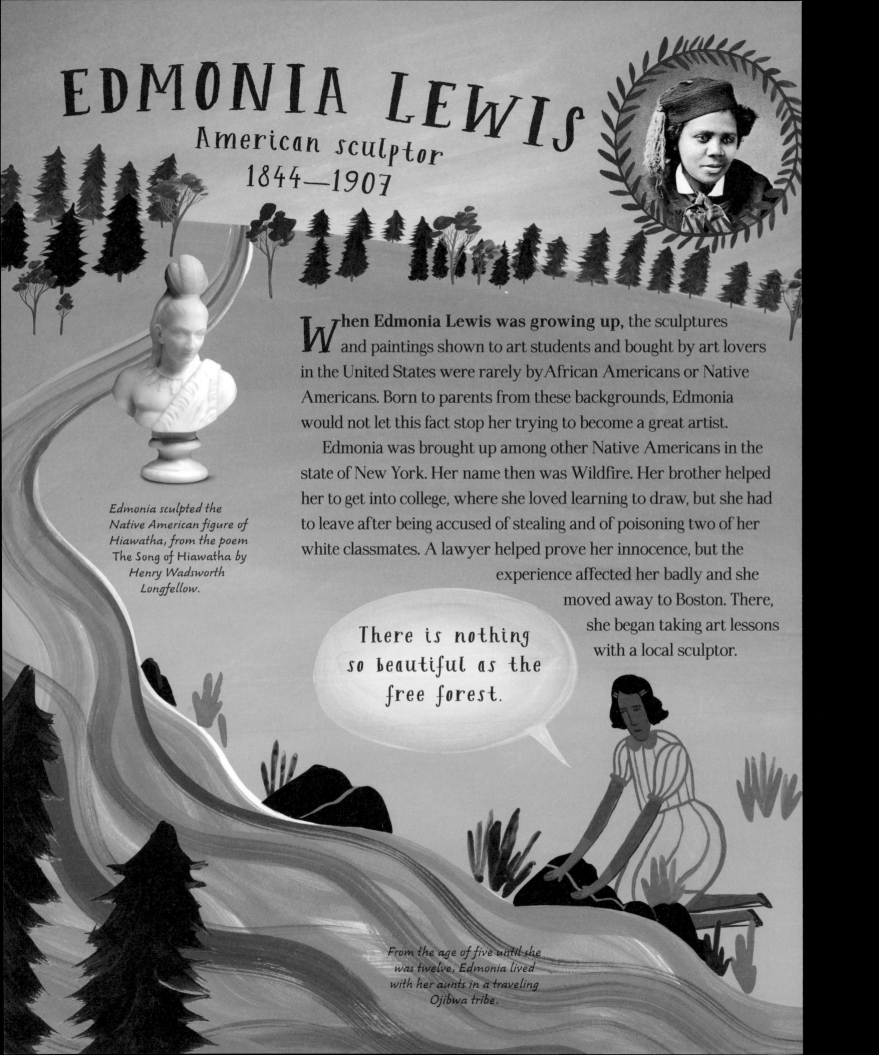

Edmonia sculpted the Native American figure of Hiawatha, from the poem The Song of Hiawatha by Henry Wadsworth Longfellow.

When Edmonia Lewis was growing up, the sculptures and paintings shown to art students and bought by art lovers in the United States were rarely by African Americans or Native Americans. Born to parents from these backgrounds, Edmonia would not let this fact stop her trying to become a great artist.

Edmonia was brought up among other Native Americans in the state of New York. Her name then was Wildfire. Her brother helped her to get into college, where she loved learning to draw, but she had to leave after being accused of stealing and of poisoning two of her white classmates. A lawyer helped prove her innocence, but the experience affected her badly and she moved away to Boston. There, she began taking art lessons with a local sculptor.

> There is nothing so beautiful as the free forest.

From the age of five until she was twelve, Edmonia lived with her aunts in a traveling Ojibwa tribe.

Classical inspiration

When Edmonia saw classical sculptures in Europe, she was inspired to create similar figures. These were smooth and realistic-looking, based on ancient Greek and Roman art.

Edmonia's African American sculptures showed enslaved people, who were usually ignored in art.

Most of Edmonia's fellow sculptors carved their work in clay, for Italian stoneworkers to copy in marble. Breaking the mold, Edmonia carved all her own work.

Sculpting a path

Edmonia's first sculptures were round portrait medals, and they were good enough to sell. With the money from these sales, Edmonia traveled to Rome, Italy, and lived near other artists, with whom she became friends. She began creating statues of famous historical and biblical figures.

Word spread about Edmonia's talent, and her studio was visited by many. Her sculpture of the ancient Egyptian queen Cleopatra was shipped to the United States and put on display in a grand exhibition. But her most important sculptures were of African American and Native American people, created in a classical European style that was usually only used to depict white people.

VINCENT VAN GOGH

Dutch painter • 1853—1890

Vincent spent a year in a hospital due to his mental illness. There, he created around 150 paintings, including Starry Night.

Now one of the most famous artists in the world, Vincent van Gogh was not successful during his life. He lived for just thirty-seven years, and only painted for ten of them. But in that short time, he produced more than two thousand paintings and drawings.

Vincent grew up among the patchwork fields of the Netherlands, with five siblings—including his beloved brother Theo. When he was old enough to leave home, he worked in France, Belgium, and England—teaching, selling art, and preaching the Christian religion. Vincent suffered from periods of depression. At the time, doctors did not know much about mental illness, so he was not treated properly.

If you truly love nature, you will find beauty everywhere.

Impasto technique

Vincent's style of thick strokes of oil paint on canvas is called impasto. He used impasto to add texture, and a sense of emotion and movement to his art.

Starry Night

One of Vincent's most famous paintings is dominated by a swirling night sky, with glowing stars and a moon in bright, contrasting yellows, oranges, and blues, over mountains, a village, and a tall, dark-green cypress tree.

Dark and starry nights

Despite his health problems, Vincent found comfort in nature, which inspired him to create paintings and drawings. He was able to express his feelings through his art, and he captured everyday life as well as landscapes. His painting style was different from others, built up with thick paint and short brushstrokes. He was inspired by other art, including Impressionism—a style that captures images of nature in bright colors. For a time, Vincent wanted to set up an artists' group, but only one artist joined him, Paul Gauguin. They had an argument, and Paul left—causing a devastated Vincent to cut off his own ear. As his illness grew worse, Vincent found comfort in his brother Theo, who encouraged him to be the artist that Theo knew he could be.

When Vincent could not sell his art, his brother Theo gave him money and paint. Vincent and Theo wrote each other many letters—in one, Vincent called Theo his only friend.

Sunflowers

As well as natural scenes, Vincent painted "still life"—specially arranged still objects from nature, such as fruit or flowers. He painted twelve famous paintings of bright sunflowers.

GEORGES SEURAT
French painter
1859—1891

Not content with just looking at pictures, Georges Seurat spent much of his time studying the science of color, and how other artists had shown it. He used his knowledge to create paintings that used color in a unique way.

Georges studied art in his home city of Paris, France. Like many artists, he learned to draw and paint by copying the paintings and sculptures of great artists. He had to stop making art for a year to serve in the French army, like other young Frenchmen, but he eagerly returned to Paris afterward. For a long time, he only made black-and-white drawings, but he also studied paintings by Eugène Delacroix, making notes on how he used color.

Georges was inspired by scenes all around him. He loved to draw people bustling around in Paris, or relaxing in the countryside outside the city.

I painted like that because I wanted to get through to something new—a kind of painting that was my own.

Divisionism

Georges figured out a way of painting colors by separating them into little dots or strokes. This style and the effects it made became known as "divisionism."

Georges went out to observe everyday life in Paris and drew sketches of what he saw. Later, he used the sketches to make paintings in his studio.

Pointillism

Tiny dots of color placed together can be seen separately up close, but from a distance they appear to mix together. Pointillism describes the technique of applying dots.

Dot to dot

In 1884, Georges began painting a huge canvas, depicting the island of La Grande Jatte on the Seine River, Paris. The painting, of Parisians enjoying themselves on a Sunday, took him two years to complete. He visited the island to study the scenery and light, and fashionably dressed models posed in his studio for the figures.

On the surface of the picture, he painted thousands of tiny dots in different colors. When looking at the painting, they seem to mix together and gleam vividly. One color theory says that when certain colors are next to each other, they make each other look brighter, and this was why Georges worked in this way.

Georges and a few other artists set up the Society of Independent Artists in Paris, to exhibit their own art. The painting above shows a figure representing liberty asking artists to take part in the society's exhibition.

57

RABINDRANATH TAGORE
Indian polymath • 1861—1941

A polymath is someone who knows about many topics. Rabindranath Tagore wrote stories, novels, poems, and dramas; he composed music; and he painted. Rabindranath was raised in a rich family that loved music and books. He preferred walks in the countryside to schoolwork, and later said that learning should be about increasing curiosity, not just being taught things. Still, he gained knowledge in a wide range of topics, from science to poetry. As an adult he wrote music and different kinds of books, including a poetry collection about devotion to God that won a Nobel Prize in Literature. He was the first person to compose national anthems for two countries—Bangladesh and India. In his sixties, he finally began to paint.

The Haida people from the Pacific Northwest of America make bold carvings of animals, such as the one above. Rabindranath painted animals in similarly stylistic (un-lifelike) ways.

Animals
Rabindranath's first drawings were spontaneous (unplanned) doodles. He turned these into pictures of imaginary animals.

Untitled art

Rabindranath's first paintings were lively and often included animals or imaginary creatures. He did not give his paintings titles because he wanted viewers to think individually about what the pictures might show or mean, based on their own ideas.

Rabindranath developed a unique painting style influenced by art from around the world, including craftwork by the Malanggan people of Papua New Guinea, Haida carvings, and woodcuts by the German expressionist artist Max Pechstein. As he grew older, he took long walks through local landscapes, often early in the morning, before dawn. He turned what he saw into mysterious-looking paintings with glowing sunrises.

Humans

People in Rabindranath's paintings often don't look quite as they do in real life. He gave them interesting outlines, or showed faces that look like masks.

रवीन्द्रनाथ ठाकुर RABINDRANATH TAGORE
1·00 1978 भारत INDIA

Rabindranath crossed out lines and words after drawing them, so his images looked accidental.

Can you see a number in the circle above? Color-blind people cannot, because they see color differently than most people. Rabindranath had this condition, which may explain the unusual and striking color combinations in his art.

59

IMPRESSIONISM

Working in around 1860, the Impressionists broke with the painting traditions of the past, which focused on making images look lifelike. Instead, they aimed to capture the light and mood of a scene. Rather than making sketches to copy in the studio, some of them painted outside.

Colorful shadows

The Impressionists used bold, vivid colors, often to show bright sunlight. Several artists avoided using black altogether, instead making their darkest and deepest tones from mixtures of dazzling colors.

Painting life

Instead of paint pictures from myths or stories, Impressionists wanted to capture everyday life. They captured the excitement of lively scenes, such as *Luncheon of the Boating Party* below, painted by Pierre-Auguste Renoir.

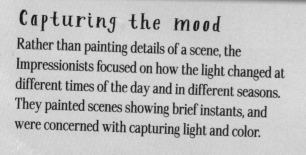

Capturing the mood

Rather than painting details of a scene, the Impressionists focused on how the light changed at different times of the day and in different seasons. They painted scenes showing brief instants, and were concerned with capturing light and color.

Missing lines

Since Impressionist artists worked quickly in loose, sketchy styles, using short brushstrokes, many of the paintings have no clear lines between objects. Instead, they appear soft and a little blurry. At the time, people were used to seeing precise brushwork, and thought these paintings looked unfinished.

If you look closely at an Impressionist painting, you will probably see broken marks of bold color. These are blended together by our eyes from farther away, in a process called "optical mixing."

The recent invention of easily portable tin tubes of paint allowed the Impressionists to paint wherever they wanted—which was often outside.

Short brushstrokes

For speed, Impressionist painters often applied short, broken brushstrokes, rather than smooth, careful marks. They built up these marks in layers to complete the image.

Flat art

Because the Impressionist painters used fewer contrasting light and dark tones than many artists before them, some of their paintings look flat, without much depth. This was different to the celebrated art of the Renaissance, and it shocked some art critics of the time.

Some Impressionists used a palette knife to layer colors on top of each other, giving the paintings texture.

LOUIS WAIN

British illustrator and painter
1860—1939

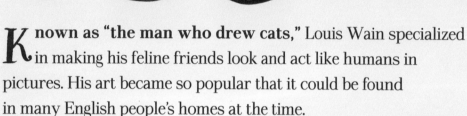

Known as "the man who drew cats," Louis Wain specialized in making his feline friends look and act like humans in pictures. His art became so popular that it could be found in many English people's homes at the time.

Born in London, UK, Louis had a cleft lip—which means his upper lip did not develop in the same way as other children's. His doctor suggested that he not go to school until he was ten years old. After that he still missed lessons, preferring to wander around London. When he was older, he studied at the West London School of Art and then became a teacher there. At twenty, his father died and Louis had to support his mother and sisters. He fell in love with his sister Emily's governess and married her. He left teaching and became a successful illustrator for magazines.

When Louis began as an illustrator, he drew detailed and realistic pictures for magazines. These mainly included country scenes, and animals that he copied closely from real life.

Emily fell ill a few years into the marriage. She was comforted by a stray black and white kitten that she and Louis rescued one night. They called him Peter.

Human cats

Louis gave his cats human behavior, as well as clothing and postures. They played instruments or cards, drank tea, and went to the opera.

Cat-ching on

Louis began drawing the family cat, Peter, and Emily encouraged him to publish the drawings. After a while, he started drawing cats standing on two legs and wearing clothes. These unique, human-like cats appeared in a Christmas issue of *The Illustrated London News*, called *A Kittens' Christmas Party*. His drawings grew in popularity, and could soon be found on packaging and postcards.

Over thirty years, Louis produced thousands of cat drawings, including the illustrations for around one hundred children's books, and the *Louis Wain Annual*, published each year from 1901 to 1915. He traveled to New York to draw comic strips of cats for newspapers, and even designed 3D ceramic cats. His love of cats led him to help multiple animal charities, and he became the chairperson of the UK's National Cat Club.

Although Louis's cat pictures were extremely popular, he remained poor. Any money he made from selling his work for businesses to use on advertisements went toward supporting his family.

Patterns

In later life, Louis became mentally ill. Some people think that the vibrant patterns in his art from that time were based on how he saw the world because of his illness.

63

HILMA AF KLINT

Swedish painter · 1862–1944

Life is a farce if a person does not serve truth.

Most of Hilma af Klint's childhood was spent at a Swedish naval academy where her father, a naval officer, was based. Each summer, her family went to stay on an island in Lake Malaren, where the beautiful scenery inspired Hilma to be creative. She spent hours studying and drawing nature. When she left school, Hilma became one of the first women to study at Stockholm's Royal Academy of Fine Arts, where she learned to paint. For doing well, she was given the use of an art studio. As well as painting, Hilma began attending séances, which are meetings where people try to contact the dead.

Hilma trained here, at the Royal Academy of Fine Arts in Stockholm, from 1887. After that she began painting landscapes and portraits in the popular realistic style of the time.

At first, Hilma painted natural-looking portraits and landscapes. From a young age, she had been fascinated by nature and botany (the scientific study of plants).

After her death, Hilma left behind more than one hundred notebooks, sketchbooks, and a dictionary explaining her own secret words.

The Five

From 1896, Hilma began meeting four female artist friends regularly. They called themselves The Five, and they tried to connect with spirits during séances and make "free-flowing" art.

Séances and shapes

At one of the séances, Hilma said she heard a voice telling her to make paintings to "proclaim a new philosophy of life." She began to make "free-flowing" drawings, which she believed were guided by spirits. These artworks were among the first modern abstract, or non-realistic, art. Using circles, spirals, and other shapes, the paintings suggested different stages of human life, including childhood and old age. Within nine years, Hilma had produced almost 200 paintings, which she called *Paintings for the Temple*. However, no one else saw her new style of work until the 1980s. Hilma would not exhibit anything, and she wrote in her will that her paintings should not be seen until long after her death.

The birth of abstract

Hilma was one of the first artists to paint modern abstract images. Instead of painting recognizable things from the real world, she painted shapes and symbols she invented in bright colors.

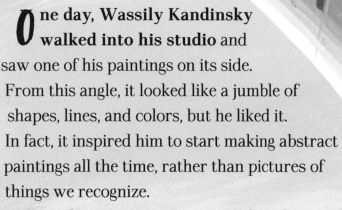

One day, **Wassily Kandinsky walked into his studio** and saw one of his paintings on its side. From this angle, it looked like a jumble of shapes, lines, and colors, but he liked it. In fact, it inspired him to start making abstract paintings all the time, rather than pictures of things we recognize.

Wassily grew up in Russia. He loved art and music, and learned to play the piano and cello at an early age. Later, he studied law at college, but when he was thirty he decided to become an artist and moved to Germany.

Wassily was inspired by colorful Russian folk art and brightly decorated houses and churches—he said entering them was like walking into a painting.

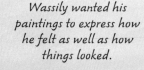

Wassily wanted his paintings to express how he felt as well as how things looked.

Moved by Monet

After seeing a painting of haystacks created with bright colors by the French Impressionist Claude Monet, Wassily began using brilliant colors in his own paintings.

WASSILY KANDINSKY
Russian painter • 1866—1944

Wassily did not always make abstract paintings. He began his career painting very realistic pictures, but even these were vividly colored.

Color and music

Wassily's paintings were influenced by the French artists known as the Impressionists and the Fauvists, who painted with bright colors. He also believed that colors, shapes, and music could express feelings, and that painting was like creating music. For example, he said that yellow had the sound of a trumpet and that green was a tuba.

As well as painting, Wassily set up an artist group called The Blue Rider, which discussed ideas about art, such as the things it should show. Their ideas influenced artists all over the world.

Wassily had a condition called synaesthesia, which meant that he "saw" colors when he heard music, and "heard" music when he painted.

Abandoning reality

Wassily was one of the first artists to paint abstract works. The influence of music on him was so great that he called quick paintings "improvisations" and more detailed works, like this one, "compositions."

ABSTRACT ART

From ancient history to the late 1800s, most artists copied things they could see. Then, several artists began creating distorted images, focusing on emotion and other invisible things. Eventually, some art became abstract—meaning that it didn't represent anything you might see in real life.

Fauvism

From 1905, a number of French artists chose to paint simply, using vivid, unnatural colors and few details to express feelings such as joy. This painting by Henri Manguin captures the happy feeling you might have on a sunny day by the shore.

Strange shapes

Some artists make abstract sculptures that might represent certain feelings. Barbara Hepworth made interesting shapes out of bronze, as shown in this artwork.

Automatic painting

Some artists in the 1920s felt that painting thoughtfully with a brush made boring art. Instead, they began painting without thinking about the marks they were making. But this method wasn't actually new—Hilma af Klint had tried it years before, with paintings such as this one.

Yellow made Wassily think of trumpet sounds, and light blue was like a flute.

Action painting

In the 1940s, some artists in the United States began experimenting with radical ways of painting, such as dripping or pouring paint rather than carefully using a brush. This was meant to help show thoughts and feelings that the artists might not know they had.

Like music

Wassily Kandinsky noticed that music made him feel emotions, and he wanted his art to have the same effect. In his paintings, such as the one shown here, he used colors, lines, and shapes that he thought were like the sounds of certain instruments.

Can you think of any feelings shown in this unknown artist's action painting?

Just color

In the 1950s and 1960s, "color field" artists covered canvases with huge areas of color, to bring out emotions in viewers. They experimented with techniques such as soaking or staining the canvases with paint.

Orange and Red on Red, by Mark Rothko, is made up of two areas of block color.

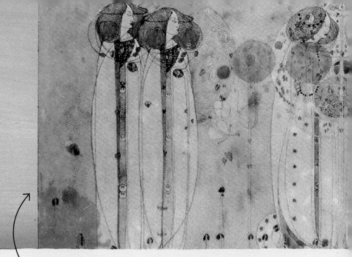

Magical art

Inspired by folklore, Celtic art, and poetry, Margaret created magical-looking watercolors and embroideries. They were delicate, made with flowing lines and jewel-like colors.

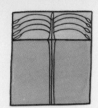 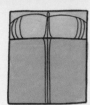 

For all sorts of interiors, Margaret created decorative painted panels, with mysterious-looking pictures and designs. She often used gesso, which is paint made from plaster.

Art isn't just pictures on walls or gleaming statues, it can also be beautifully designed rooms—like those by Margaret Macdonald Mackintosh. She was especially creative when working with others.

Margaret was born in England and moved to Glasgow, Scotland, in her twenties. She and her sister Frances studied at the Glasgow School of Art, where they met Charles Rennie Mackintosh and Herbert McNair. The sisters set up an art studio, and then Frances married Herbert and Margaret married Charles. The group designed metalwork, book illustrations, room interiors, and furniture, in what became called the "Modern Style."

Margaret and Charles worked together designing all kinds of rooms, such as in cafés and homes. They worked with wood, metal, and glass.

MARGARET MACDONALD MACKINTOSH

British designer • 1864—1933

Together with his wife, her sister, and her sister's husband, Charles Rennie Mackintosh formed part of the artistic group "The Four."

Born in Glasgow, the young Charles became an apprentice of a local architect and signed up to evening art classes at the Glasgow School of Art. From there, he joined an architectural firm, and soon won an award for his building designs. The money he was given with the award funded a trip to Europe, where he drew buildings. On his own and with The Four, he designed many things, including lights, posters, and buildings. One of his most famous building designs is the Glasgow School of Art, where he had once studied.

The duo designed everything. Visitors to the tea room sat on Mackintosh chairs, drank tea from specially designed cups, and ate with Mackintosh cutlery.

Mackintosh chairs

Charles designed elegant furniture inspired by nature. His popular chairs are all tall and slim, and every one is different. They look simple, but are made with shapes that fit together like jigsaws.

CHARLES RENNIE MACKINTOSH

Scottish designer • 1868—1928

71

HENRI MATISSE
French painter, sculptor, and cut-out artist
1869—1954

Henri Matisse was on the path to becoming a lawyer before he decided to follow his heart and take up art. He went on to create brand-new styles of painting and collage.

It was suffering from appendicitis that sparked Henri's decision to begin painting, at the age of twenty. His mother gave him some paints while he recovered, and he decided it was all he wanted to do. He went to learn his craft in Paris, where he discovered Impressionism and the work of Paul Cézanne and Georges Seurat. These great artists painted differently than the figurative (lifelike) artists Henri was used to. He began experimenting with vivid, unnatural colors, applied loosely onto his canvases.

ART STUDENTS COPYING PICTURES AT THE LOUVRE, PARIS

At the Louvre Museum in Paris, Henri and countless other artists learned to paint by copying the artwork there. These paintings were figurative, since many art experts made fun of Impressionism at first.

Fauvism

This artwork by Albert Marquet includes bright colors and free brushstrokes. It was inspired by Henri's new style of painting, which became known as "Fauvism," from the French word *"fauves,"* meaning "wild beasts."

Impressionism is the newspaper of the soul.

In his eighties, Henri became ill and could not paint. Instead, from his bed, he cut out pieces of painted paper and asked his assistant to stick them down where he wanted. These were his first cut-out artworks.

Creative competition

Henri bonded over art with great figures, such as Auguste Renoir, who shared his love of color and beauty. His friendship with Pablo Picasso was rockier. They became artistic rivals.

Henri experimented with techniques such as Cubism and Pointillism, but his own lively, bright style suited him best. He aimed to express joyful feelings with his paintings, and said he wanted everyone to enjoy it, "like a good armchair." He was also eager to make art that looked new and different—not just in his paintings, but in sculptures that showed people in abstract (non-realistic) ways, and with his famous paper cut-outs.

Cut-outs

Henri's cut-outs included simple figures and bold colors. This cut-out shows Icarus, a mythical figure. In the myth, Icarus makes himself wax wings, which melt when he flies too close to the sun.

PIET MONDRIAN
Dutch painter • 1872—1944

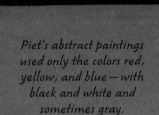

Piet's abstract paintings used only the colors red, yellow, and blue—with black and white and sometimes gray.

The gridlike paintings that **Piet Mondrian** is known for today are unrecognizable from the lifelike landscapes of his early career. After training in a traditional, naturalistic style, he became inspired by the exciting new ideas of abstract art.

Piet grew up in the Netherlands and studied art in Amsterdam, before becoming a painter and art teacher. But Paris, France, was where all the exciting new art was being made, so Piet traveled there. In Paris he discovered the art of Cubism, in which artists distort objects to show different viewpoints. Piet soon began experimenting with his own paintings. When the First World War forced him to return to the Netherlands, he used his knowledge of new art to help produce an art magazine called *De Stijl* (*The Style*).

Early work

Piet's early paintings were of the countryside around Amsterdam. They were paintings of nature and some buildings, including trees, windmills, rivers, houses, and skies.

Becoming less real

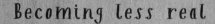

After being inspired by Cubism in Paris, Piet's paintings became more abstract. He made everything simpler, including his lines and colors.

The new style

De Stijl became a new abstract art movement, also called Neoplasticism, and Piet was one of its leaders. The art was meant to show the idea that everything in the universe has a natural balance. These ideas could be used in many of the arts—such as architecture, or building design, and fashion.

After the First World War, Piet moved back to Paris, where he created his abstract paintings. Through them, he aimed to express the harmony, peace, and rhythms of the universe by reducing his colors and lines to their "purist," or most basic. He no longer tried to make pictures that looked like the real world.

The new plastic art

Neoplasticism means "the new plastic art." Its artists believed the universe has a spiritual harmony, which means there is more to the world than we can see.

In his abstract paintings, all Piet's lines are either vertical or horizontal, and cross each other at right angles.

Piet would only use straight lines in his later abstract paintings. He carefully drew them without using a ruler!

"It is not important to make many pictures, but that I have one picture right."

Piet read about spiritual ideas. He joined the Theosophical Society— a spiritual organization based on some of the ideas of Buddhism—and this helped to influence his work.

Paula Modersohn-Becker was born in Dresden, Germany, then moved with her family to Bremen. She began to learn about art as a teenager, and later studied in Berlin, Germany, and Paris, France—even though it wasn't easy for girls to study art at that time.

Her parents wanted her to be a teacher and to stop work once she married. Instead, she became one of Germany's most important early Expressionists. Expressionism is a style of art that shows real objects, but not in a lifelike way, instead focusing on the emotions they make you feel.

Paula was influenced by French Post-Impressionist artists, such as Paul Cézanne, who painted with many small brushstrokes to build up the look of solid shapes, as in Cézanne's artwork above.

Some of Paula's favorite subjects to paint were women and, in particular, mothers and babies.

PAULA MODERSOHN-BECKER
German painter • 1876–1907

Paula returned to Paris several times in her life. There, she could paint and study great paintings in galleries.

Original work

Paula went to live in a small village named Worpswede in northern Germany, where a community of artists met and painted outside. However, Paula preferred painting the local people rather than the landscape. Deciding her work was too different from the other artists, she moved to Paris where a lot of original art was being produced.

In 1901, she returned to Worpswede, but even after that she often came back to Paris to develop her art. Sadly, Paula died when she was just thirty-one after having a baby.

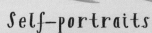

Self-portraits

Paula is now well-known for her portraits and self-portraits. Her pictures of people didn't try to be lifelike, but instead showed their inner feelings.

On her return to Worpswede, Paula married another artist, Otto Modersohn.

Artists' colony

Paula's friend Clara Westhoff, a sculptor, also lived in Worpswede with her husband, Rainer Maria Rilke, a famous poet. Together the artists shared ideas.

JEAN ARP

German–French sculptor, painter, and poet • 1886—1966

In 1926, Jean, his wife, Sophie, and another artist were asked to design the inside of Café Aubette, a building in Strasbourg with dancehalls and restaurants. They covered the walls in colorful shapes.

In the early twentieth century, artists started making nonsense art, using silly or odd things. One of the founders of this new style was Jean Arp.

Born in Strasbourg, which was then part of Germany but is now in France, Jean trained as an artist in three different cities—his hometown, the German city of Weimar, and Paris, France. He learned to create sculptures, poetry, and paintings, and became known for his surreal style.

In 1912, in Munich, he contributed drawings to *Der Blaue Reiter* (The Blue Rider), an artists' group that created expressive, abstract art. During World War I, he lived in Zürich, Switzerland, where he helped develop a new type of art—Dada.

Sculptures

Jean became best known for his biomorphic sculptures. These are abstract forms that resemble natural shapes such as plants or vegetables—sculpted in stone or bronze.

Changing style

Jean made abstract paintings, drawings, collages, and prints, changing his style quite often. Many of his early works were made up of straight lines and angles. Later, they featured softer shapes.

78

Set design

Sophie designed stage sets for performances and puppets, using shapes and bright colors. The puppets and patterns expressed her understanding of rhythm from years of dancing.

Influenced by her training in textile design, Sophie created paintings using vivid colors and simple shapes in different arrangements and patterns.

Her creative mind and unusual view of the world led Sophie Taeuber-Arp to make many different types of art. She produced sculptures, textiles, furniture, interior (room) designs, buildings, costumes, and dances.

She went to art and dance school in Switzerland, and studied painting, textile design, and dance. During World War I, she moved back to Switzerland, where she met Jean Arp in 1915. They married and, like him, she became part of the Dada movement. She is best known today for her abstract works of art based on geometric shapes and bold colors.

Textiles

Sophie made textiles to hang on walls like paintings, which was unusual at the time. She embroidered her textiles with abstract patterns.

SOPHIE TAEUBER-ARP

swiss multi-format artist • 1889—1943

CLEMENTINE HUNTER

American painter • 1886—1988

With her eyes always open to the world around her, Clementine Hunter had many memories to draw from when she began making art in her fifties. She painted everyday life on the leafy plantation where she lived in Louisiana.

Clementine began working as a farm laborer on the Melrose plantation from a young age, picking cotton and pecan nuts. In her forties, she began working in the main house as a cook and housekeeper. Melrose became an artists' colony around this time, where famous artists could stay and work. They left old tubes of paint around, which Clementine started using.

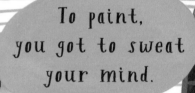

> To paint, you got to sweat your mind.

Clementine's grandsons, James and Frank, loved her paintings. She taught them to paint, and they became artists, too.

Painting her life

Clementine painted brightly colored images of what life was like for many Black people in the southern United States. Among other things, she showed cotton-picking, chores, and weddings.

Clementine and many other Black people in the American South were poor and lived in small houses. This was because they were not given the same opportunities in education and jobs as white people.

Like most people in America at the time, Clementine was a Christian. She celebrated Christian ceremonies, such as baptisms and funerals, and holy days such as Christmas.

Melrose

Plantations (large farms) often used enslaved people as labor. For most of her life, Clementine lived and worked on the Melrose cotton plantation. After working all day, she painted at night, when everyone else was asleep.

Making up for lost time

Clementine began painting as much as she could, on any surface she could find. She created pictures showing different experiences she remembered, such as community celebrations and jobs she had done.

Wealthy friends of Melrose's owner, Cammie Henry, were impressed by Clementine's work and offered to help her keep painting. In particular, François Mignon gave Clementine paints and materials and organized exhibitions of her paintings in a local shop. Since she was never taught to write, Clementine signed her work with a backward *C* and an *H*, joined together.

Clementine's cooking impressed her friend François Mignon, who asked her to write a cookbook with him. She agreed, and drew the illustrations for the book, too.

Clementine didn't spend all her time working and painting—she also enjoyed playing games! One of her paintings shows people playing cards at a table.

Although Clementine is now famous, she was poor for most of her life. She sometimes made money by charging people a small amount to see her paintings.

25 cents to look

81

FOLK ART

Rather than being made to be exhibited in galleries or at exhibitions, folk art is usually produced for practical purposes. The skilled artists tend to be people working in their homes in small communities, away from large cities. They might be shepherds, sailors, or professional craftspeople, and are usually taught their art form by family members or others in the community.

Useable

Folk art is usually made to be useful rather than to be simply hung on a wall. It might be a household item, such as a rug or an item of furniture. Or, it could be wearable art, such as clothing or jewelry. It could even be a musical instrument or a moveable toy.

Wearable crafts

In some societies, folk artists make their own traditional costumes, often including both clothing and jewelry, to be worn for local festivals or religious or spiritual rituals. These distinct costumes rarely change over the years, so they can act like a kind of time capsule.

Local materials

Just as folk artists create locally developed styles of art, they also mainly use materials that can be found nearby. These can be anything from bright gold found underground, to straw, wood, and sheep's wool.

Motifs

Almost all folk art features symbols and motifs (repeated images), which tend to be from the artist's community. These motifs are often brightly colored images or patterns, that may be simplified versions of an animal or a natural object, such as a flower or plant.

Handmade

Many folk artists do not use machines, but make their art by hand. They often use traditional skills that have been practiced for a long time in their community, such as wood carving, pottery, weaving, or embroidery.

Painting

Folk art has influenced some well-known artists—including a few of the painters in this book. Folk artists themselves have also become known outside of their communities because of their talents. In the twentieth century, the folk painter John Kane became widely known in the United States for his landscapes.

Traditional

A community can develop traditions based around folk artworks. In Wales, for example, intricately carved wooden love spoons are made as gifts for loved ones and are meant to be displayed on a wall. These were first made in the seventeenth century, and are still being given today.

PABLO PICASSO

Spanish sculptor and painter • 1881—1973

It's easy to spot a **Pablo Picasso** painting if you know what to look for. He co-founded the Cubist movement, which showed uniquely distorted figures.

Pablo grew up in Spain and went to art schools in the Spanish cities of Barcelona and Madrid. After painting realistically for a short while, he soon turned to experimenting with abstract (un-lifelike) forms. At nineteen, while Pablo was living in Paris, France, his art was affected by the death of a close friend. Pablo became dreadfully sad, and would only make blue paintings of forlorn subjects. After this "Blue Period" came his "Rose Period," featuring cheerier, warmer colors such as pink. Next came Cubism.

"Every child is an artist."

Pablo painted portraits that were unrecognizable from their subjects. They were often shown as a series of curved or angled shapes, in natural or unnatural colors.

Cubism

Started by Pablo and Georges Braque in France in 1907, Cubism depicts several viewpoints of a subject at once. This makes the subject look as if it is made up of different shapes.

LYUBOV POPOVA
Russian painter • 1889—1924

As Cubism grew in popularity, artists began changing it to create new movements. Lyubov Popova was one of the artists working and experimenting at this exciting time.

One of the first movements Lyubov became involved with was Cubo-Futurism, a mixture of French Cubism and Italian Futurism, which depicted modern themes such as technology. She then began painting in the Suprematist style—a kind of abstract art that included geometric (angular) shapes and lines. Always changing her style, she also became known for her unnatural-looking Constructivist works of art.

Lyubov often used thick paint with vibrant colors in rigid, abstract styles. Unnatural shapes fill these canvases, though she also loved more lifelike styles, such as Russian icons (paintings of religious figures).

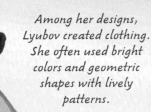

Among her designs, Lyubov created clothing. She often used bright colors and geometric shapes with lively patterns.

Constructivism

In the 1910s, a Russian art movement began that aimed to reflect the modern world, which was filled with plain, practical buildings with simple shapes, such as factories. Lyubov designed the set of a play in this style.

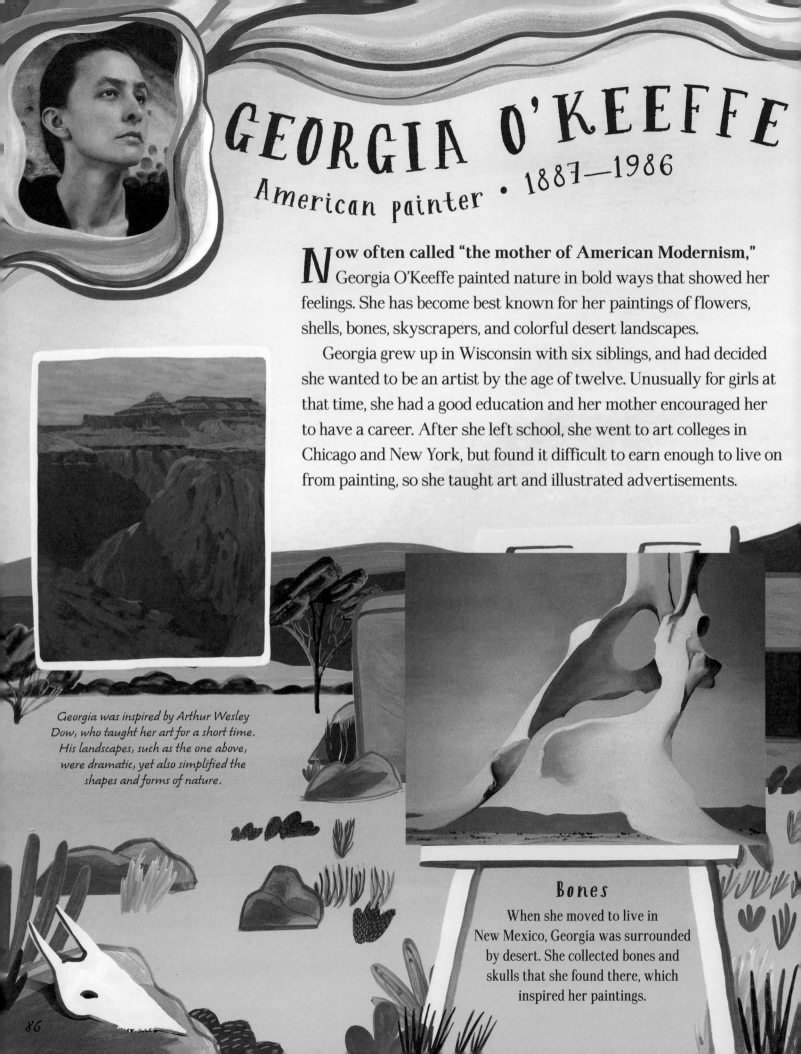

GEORGIA O'KEEFFE
American painter • 1887—1986

Now often called "the mother of American Modernism," Georgia O'Keeffe painted nature in bold ways that showed her feelings. She has become best known for her paintings of flowers, shells, bones, skyscrapers, and colorful desert landscapes.

Georgia grew up in Wisconsin with six siblings, and had decided she wanted to be an artist by the age of twelve. Unusually for girls at that time, she had a good education and her mother encouraged her to have a career. After she left school, she went to art colleges in Chicago and New York, but found it difficult to earn enough to live on from painting, so she taught art and illustrated advertisements.

Georgia was inspired by Arthur Wesley Dow, who taught her art for a short time. His landscapes, such as the one above, were dramatic, yet also simplified the shapes and forms of nature.

Bones

When she moved to live in New Mexico, Georgia was surrounded by desert. She collected bones and skulls that she found there, which inspired her paintings.

City to open sky

In the 1920s, Georgia became the first female painter to gain respect and interest in New York's art world, and this helped her to influence the development of modern art in America. As well as oil paints, she used watercolors and made charcoal sketches. Without telling Georgia, a friend sent some of her drawings to the famous photographer Alfred Stieglitz in New York. He displayed them in his gallery and then became friends with Georgia. Eight years later, they married.

In New York, Georgia painted huge pictures of close-up flowers and skyscrapers. After Alfred died, Georgia moved to the desert state of New Mexico, where she painted the skies, vast landscapes, and natural objects.

Flowers

During the 1920s, Georgia created large paintings of close-up flowers. She said painting flowers in such a big scale made their beauty impossible to ignore, causing people to stop and think.

> When you take a flower in your hand and really look at it, it's your world for the moment.

In New Mexico, Georgia never tired of painting the colorful hills, cliffs, rivers, mountains, and rocks, and the changing light effects. She called this landscape "the Faraway."

87

COLLAGE

From the start of the twentieth century, some professional artists began using collage. Rather than painting or sculpting, they glued various materials on to surfaces, creating a radical style of art that had never been seen before. This was called "collage" from the French word "coller," meaning to glue or stick together.

Painting

Some collages also include painted elements. From 1912, Georges Braque and Pablo Picasso began gluing other materials on to their paintings, such as pieces of newsprint, wallpaper, string, and rope.

Found images

Some artists make collages using things they find around them. These could be found anywhere, such as pages from magazines, pieces of fabric, or dried rice or pasta. It could even be litter from the street—for example used tickets, leaflets, or old newspapers. These would all be arranged and stuck down on a surface.

Artists might use newspapers in their collages to draw people's attention to serious events talked about on the pages, such as war.

Fabric

Colored scraps of fabric can be cut and arranged into striking artworks. Some artists that experiment with fabric in their collages see this as a way to protect the environment, by reusing shabby old clothing that may otherwise be headed to the landfill.

Drawing

Some early twentieth-century artists combined collage with the more traditional European art form of drawing. Juan Gris stuck down materials such as newspapers, wallpaper, and colored paper, then drew on them, often with crayons.

Today, some artists use computers to create digital collages. They crop, or cut, sections from digital images and put them together to make interesting art.

3D art

Not all collage is flat— some artists make 3D collages called assemblages, like this one by Carl Worner. They can take many forms, such as a collection of thrown-away objects stuck together, or items arranged carefully in a box or other container.

Not all art is made on purpose! Some artists spot an image in their home or out and about that could be seen as art. Such images include collage—such as a wall with layers of torn posters.

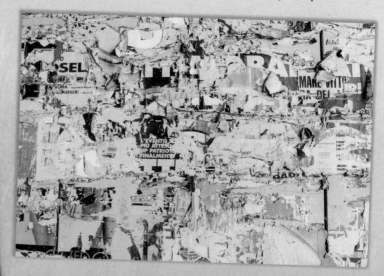

19

AFTER 1900

By the beginning of the twentieth century, much of the art found in galleries was about experimenting and exploring the artists' own ideas. Some artists tried out new ways of showing reality, while others wanted to show their innermost feelings, or what they thought about the world and life around them.

PRINCESS FAHRELNISSA ZEID

Turkish painter • 1901—1991

In Baghdad, Fahrelnissa saw women in colorful, traditional dress through her windows. The colors, broken up by the lines in the window frames, helped inspire her abstract work.

Growing up in Turkey and studying art in France led Fahrelnissa Zeid to mix Turkish and European styles of art. She created huge portraits and large, colorful, abstract paintings that now span entire walls in world-famous art galleries.

Fahrelnissa's father held an important job in the Turkish government, but he found time to enjoy the arts and literature and encouraged his children to do the same. Fahrelnissa eagerly did so. She was often found painting as a child, and went to art school when she was old enough. She married at the age of nineteen and the couple honeymooned in Venice , where she visited galleries and fell in love with the Baroque and other European art styles. She returned to Europe in 1928 to study painting in Paris, France.

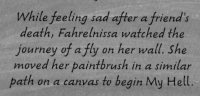

While feeling sad after a friend's death, Fahrelnissa watched the journey of a fly on her wall. She moved her paintbrush in a similar path on a canvas to begin My Hell.

92

Art all around

Fahrelnissa created large artworks, some more than 5m (16ft) wide. She liked to be surrounded by her work, and sometimes pinned paintings to the ceiling or wrapped them around walls.

Painting herself better

A few years later, having divorced her first husband and married an Iraqi prince, she began to suffer from depression. This means she felt sad and hopeless for long periods of time. She went to the hospital to see if doctors could treat the illness, and they said focusing on painting might help.

She joined a group of Turkish artists creating exciting new art, and they exhibited together. Next, she put on her first solo exhibition at her home. Now in her forties, she began to gradually make her art less figurative, combining abstract shapes with more realistic images. Finally, she started creating the colorful, abstract artworks she is most famous for—look out for her paintings that appear as though you're seeing them through a kaleidoscope.

"Often, I am aware of what I have painted only when the canvas is at last finished."

This picture shows Fahrelnissa at home in Amman, Jordan, in the 1980s. She is signing a book written about her work by a French author called André Parinaud.

93

Climbing through the rubble of a bombed city and crouching with soldiers in trenches, Gerda Taro risked her life to take photographs during the Spanish Civil War. Sadly, she would become the first female photojournalist to be killed during a war.

Gerda Pohorylle was born in Stuttgart, Germany, and grew up at the sane time as a new political party, the Nazis, began to gain popularity. They were elected as the new government, and started to pass laws so that Jewish people, such as, Gerda were persecuted (treated cruelly). A fearless Gerda gave out leaflets against them, which led to her arrest. When she was 23, Gerda and her family had to leave Germany because it was becoming too dangerous for them to live there.

When the Nazi Party took control of Germany, many Jewish people fled the country for their safety. Gerda's parents went to Palestine and her brothers to England—she never saw them again.

In 2007, boxes of Civil War photographs were found in Mexico. They were by Gerda, Robert, and David Seymour, and had been smuggled out of Europe during World War Two.

Robert Capa

It was risky to have a Jewish name in 1930s Europe, so Gerda and Endre invented an imaginary photographer, Robert Capa, and said their work was by him. Later, Gerda made up 'Taro' for her work.

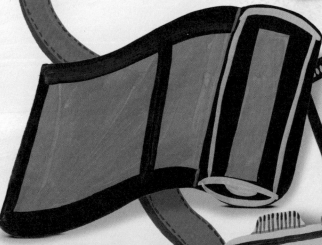

GERDA TARO
German–Jewish photographer
1910—1937

The Spanish Civil War

The Spanish Civil War lasted from 1936–1939. Gerda took photos of soldiers fighting in battles and people living in bombed cities. In the photo below, she captured women training to fight.

The little blonde

Now in Paris, France, Gerda met the Hungarian photojournalist Endre Friedmann, who began to go by the name Robert Capa. He taught her photography and she became his personal assistant.

When the Spanish Civil War broke out in 1936, Gerda, Robert, and another photographer traveled to Barcelona in Spain. The Spanish people became used to seeing Gerda snapping away with her camera, and nicknamed her *La pequeña rubia* (The little blonde). Together, she and Robert took photos of the war that were published in important magazines in Switzerland, France, and England, and soon in international newspapers, too. She was out trying to take more photographs of the Civil War when a tank crashed into her car. She died from her injuries, aged just twenty-seven.

There are three European streets named after Gerda. These are in Paris, where she was buried, Stuttgart, and Madrid, Spain.

13ᵉ Arrᵗ

RUE GERDA TARO

1910—1937
PREMIÈRE FEMME PHOTOJOURNALISTE
MORTE DANS L'EXERCICE DE SON MÉTIER.
PENDANT LA GUERRE D'ESPAGNE

LOUISE BOURGEOIS

French–American sculptor

1911—2010

Little Louise Bourgeois was often busy in her parents' tapestry studio in Paris, France—helping to weave, sew, and repair tapestries. However, her childhood was not always pleasant. When she was just two, her father went away to fight in the First World War, which raged across Europe and lasted four long years. Toward the end of the war, her beloved mother was bedridden with a bad case of the flu, and it was around this time that her parents' relationship worsened. All of these events took their toll on Louise, making her worry often. When she was at university, studying math, her worst fears came true when her mother died. But Louise decided to channel her emotions into art—swapping the study of math for learning how to paint.

Louise used found objects, such as mirrors, for her sculptures. These are objects or pieces of objects that artists find and use in their art.

Louise used fabric, such as pieces of clothing, for many of her sculptures. For example, she stuffed pairs of tights and then sewed or fixed them into strange shapes.

Maman

One of Louise's sculptures inspired by her mother was a towering, 30 ft (9 m)-tall steel spider called *Maman*—French for "Mom." Louise said spiders were weavers, and that they were clever, helpful, and protective—like her mother.

Super sculptures

At an exhibition of her work, Louise met an American art historian named Robert Goldwater. They quickly fell in love, married, and moved to New York City. Here, Louise realized that sculptures were a powerful way to express her strong emotions and memories. She began sculpting, using various materials and methods.

Louise would never forget her mother, who she called her best friend, and was often inspired by her to create artwork. She was also influenced to produce ever-bigger works of art by the gigantic skyscrapers of New York City. Other sculptures were made with objects she collected. Until her death at the age of ninety-eight, Louise poured her heart into countless sculptures, paintings, books, drawings, prints, and installations.

Louise's art often looks like lumpy, misshapen human bodies. These artworks were inspired by Louise's memories of when she had felt hurt, and show how we are affected by experiences.

To be an artist, you need to exist in a world of silence.

In the 1990s, Louise created "Cells." These are large sculptures that look like rooms or cages, filled with objects that she had collected. Some are big enough to go inside.

Drawing things

Most people think of pencils when they think of drawing. However, there are many more materials that can be used to draw with, such as charcoal and pens. Each of these materials creates distinct types of drawings—the lines might be thick or thin, or smudged or sharp. Find out which materials do what below.

Graphite pencils create gray lines and are graded by how soft (smudgy) or hard they are, from 9B to 9H.

Graphite sticks can be soft or hard. Soft graphite is good for blending and covering large surfaces.

Colored pencils use wax or oil to make the core, instead of graphite. Water can be added to some to turn them into a paint-like material.

Thick, dark charcoal was first used by prehistoric humans. It is made from certain burned materials, such as willow twigs.

Chalk pastels can be hard or soft. They can be pale or bold and bright, and can be layered or used sparingly.

Oil pastels make thick, smooth marks and can be blended by layering, rather than smudging.

Ballpoint pens create smooth, flowing marks and can be used to make a range of tones.

Felt-tip pens and markers are used by some artists to make hatching (lines) or stippling (dots) to show tones.

ART MATERIALS

Art can be made from any material you could think of, though some are easier to find than others! Traditionally, most artists have used pencils, charcoal, pens, and paints. However, many artists today use other materials, such as film, electricity, food, or garbage. They have even painted or photographed their own bodies.

Paints and ink

Delicate watercolors, smooth and buttery oil paints, opaque (not see-through) gouache, vibrant acrylics, and translucent (semi see-through) colored inks have all been used by artists to create stunning paintings.

Indian inks come in rich colors.

Acrylic inks are thin and spread easily.

 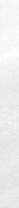  

Acrylic paint dries quite quickly.

Oil paint takes longer than acrylic paint to dry.

Gouache is used with water, but it is more opaque than watercolor.

Watercolor paints can be transparent (see-through), soft and delicate, or bright and bold.

Sculpting stuff

Sculpture can be completely 3D—called "in the round"—or a raised image attached to a background—called "in relief." Artists often use materials such as clay, wood, metal, or stone. Wood, clay, and stone are usually carved into shape, using machinery or handheld tools. Metal tends to be heated until it softens enough to be shaped.

Stainless steel

Iron

Bronze

Bronze with patina

Soapstone is soft and easily carved.

Sandstone sits near the middle of the scale of hardness for rocks.

Granite is extremely hard—so it doesn't wear easily.

Limewood is soft and smooth, making it easy to carve.

Earthenware clay comes from the ground, and is flexible and durable.

Porcelain clay is white, and made from different natural clays mixed together.

Stoneware clay is strong and useful for outdoor sculpture.

Pine is soft and easy to carve, like limewood, but it also comes in darker colors.

Moldable materials

Rather than be carved, sculpted, drawn, or painted onto a surface, some materials can be melted into liquid form and poured into molds. When they cool and harden, they take the shape of the mold. Some soft metals work like this, such as bronze and gold, but there is also resin, wax, and more. Sculptures made of these materials are made by skilled adult artists, since the process involves hot liquids that give off fumes and can be dangerous.

Reddish-brown mahogany has been carved into works of art by many craftspeople.

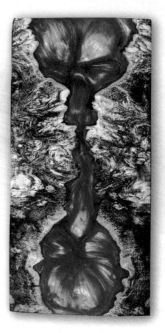

Resin is a liquid when warm, so it can take any shape. When it cools, it turns solid.

Dark brown walnut was a popular wood used for detailed religious sculptures in medieval Germany.

Wax is produced by bees to make their hives—but some artists melt and reform it to create sculpture.

JACKSON POLLOCK
American painter • 1912—1956

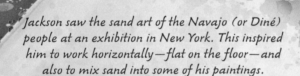

Jackson saw the sand art of the Navajo (or Diné) people at an exhibition in New York. This inspired him to work horizontally—flat on the floor—and also to mix sand into some of his paintings.

In the 1940s, American artist Jackson Pollock shocked people with his new art. In these artworks, he splashed paint onto each canvas, and he became a leading Abstract Expressionist. This style of painting doesn't depict lifelike objects, but is colorful and lively.

Jackson grew up in the western United States and didn't enjoy school—being expelled more than once. He loved painting though, and became fascinated by the art of the Indigenous peoples in America. In 1930, he moved to New York to study.

One of the earliest Abstract Expressionists was Armenian-American artist Arshile Gorky. His colorful paintings are full of unusual shapes and influenced many other artists.

Working horizontally

Unlike most painters, who work with their canvases held upright on easels, Jackson put his huge, blank canvases on the floor. This way he could work on them from every angle.

> The painting has a life of its own. I try to let it come through.

Turning off his mind

At first, Jackson painted things from real life, but from 1943, he began creating abstract "action paintings." They were unlike any other paintings produced before. He laid his large canvases on the floor of his studio and walked around each one, dripping, flinging, and pouring paint on them. He did this directly from paint cans, or with sticks and brushes. Sometimes, he even pushed the paint around with his shoes! Most of the time, while he worked, he tried not to think, so that whatever he produced came from his unconscious mind.

Drip painting

With his new techniques, Jackson changed painting forever. He said that by applying paint to the canvas without thinking, his art was created by great forces, coming through him from the universe.

SALVADOR DALÍ
Spanish painter • 1904—1989

When he was just a young boy, Spanish artist Salvador Dalí declared that he would be "the genius Dalí"—someone who would be known for his extraordinary talent. He exhibited his first landscape painting on a postcard at the age of six, and held an entire art exhibition when he was thirteen. At school, Salvador was often in trouble. He spent a lot of time doodling, grew his hair long—which was rare for a boy to do at the time—and wore unusual clothes. He continued to stand out from the crowd after he became a student at the School of Fine Arts, in Madrid, from which he was expelled—twice: first, for organizing a protest against his favorite teacher being fired, and second, for not taking an exam, because he said he knew more about art than his teachers! He left the school and traveled to Paris. There, he met his hero, the artist Pablo Picasso, and tried out different painting styles. He settled on painting his dreams and thoughts—in a style called Surrealism.

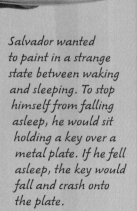

Salvador wanted to paint in a strange state between waking and sleeping. To stop himself from falling asleep, he would sit holding a key over a metal plate. If he fell asleep, the key would fall and crash onto the plate.

Once, Salvador gave a lecture while wearing a diving suit and holding two Irish wolfhounds and a billiard cue. No one could hear him through the helmet!

Surrealism

In this style of art, artists aim to express ideas from their unconscious (unawake) minds, or from their dreams. Surrealist artworks might feature imaginary landscapes, such as Salvador's *The Persistence of Memory*, shown here.

Salvador created fashion designs, magazine covers, and advertising logos—including the Chupa Chups lollipop logo still used today.

Surreal suppers

Salvador became known for throwing creative dinner parties with his wife, Gala. These were banquets in fancy dress with animals such as monkeys wandering around. Unusual food was served from vessels such as shoes. As well as paintings and dinner parties, Salvador made many other types of art, including furniture, such as a lip-shaped sofa, and the design of a museum building dedicated to him in his hometown.

At one party, live frogs hopped out of a silver dish!

Cartridge paper
Handmade paper
Sugar paper
Canvas
Chipboard
MDF wood

Supports

A surface on which to make art is called a support. Artists who want to create a drawing, painting, or print would choose this type of equipment—but what support should they go for? They might want a smooth piece of cartridge paper, which is useful for drawing on; a roughly textured handmade paper that affects the look of marks made on it; or a sturdy piece of MDF wood that doesn't crease.

Drawing tools

The sort of tool an artist uses for drawing can have a huge effect on how their art turns out. They might want sharp or blurred lines, or thicker or thinner marks.

Paper can be rolled tightly and sharpened like a pencil to make a handy tool called a stump or torchon. Pressed onto some marks, such as those made by chalk, it can be used for smudging.

All kinds of ink pens can be used for drawing. Dip pens are dipped into ink before being used to make smooth lines.

EQUIPMENT

T**o make art,** artists first need to gather his or her tools—or equipment. Artists choose equipment based on the kind of art they want to create. They might want to paint or draw something, which requires a surface on which to make marks. If they want to make 3D art, then they'll need tools with which to cut or shape materials.

Sharp tools, such as scissors, are often used to cut up materials or to slice holes or shapes out of art.

Erasers and fixatives

Some tools are used on marks that have already been made. An eraser can be used to blend colors or make an area of a drawing lighter. A see-through fixative is often sprayed onto art made with smudgeable materials, to stop it from smudging. This process is called "setting" or "fixing."

A small eraser is better for smaller marks.

Rather than being rubbed across a drawing, putty erasers can be squashed into a particular shape and pressed onto a drawing to lighten an area or remove marks.

WINSOR & NEWTON™

PROFESSIONAL FIXATIVE
FIXATIF PROFESSIONNEL
FIJATIVO PROFESIONAL
FISSATIVO PROFESSIONALE
PROFESSIONAL FIXATIV

PROTECTS DRAWINGS FROM SMUDGING & DUST.
PROTÈGE LES DESSINS DES TACHES ET DE LA POUSSIÈRE.
PROTEJE LOS DIBUJOS DE POLVO Y MANCHAS.
PROTEGGE I DISEGNI DALLA POLVERE E DALLE SBAVATURE.
SCHÜTZT ZEICHNUNGEN VOR VERSCHMIEREN & STAUB.

150 ml e NET WT 108 g 3.8 oz

Palettes and knives

Artists working with paint need tools to apply it. A palette is a surface on which to place chosen paints, ready to be added to the artwork. A palette knife is a tool used for adding paint to the palette or to apply it thickly and smoothly to the painting.

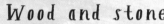
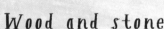

Wood and stone

For thousands of years, artists have been using tools such as chisels to carve wood and stone artworks. These tools have pointed or flat ends that can be hammered into the material to gouge out lines or chunks. Many artists still use these today, but they also have the choice of modern equipment such as electric saws and drills.

Modeling tools

When modeling or sculpting soft materials, such as clay, artists need more delicate tools than for wood or stone. These tools might be pointy or flat, or smooth or textured, depending on what the artist wants the artwork to look like.

Flat wood chisel

Wood gouge

Claw/tooth chisel

Stone punch

Brushes

Many artists prefer using brushes for painting, which are made from a collection of human-made or natural bristles attached to a handle. A brush can be thick or thin, or flat or pointed, to make wide or narrow marks. Brushes also come in different levels of stiffness—stiffer brushes are often used to create textured paintings using thick paint.

Pointed brushes are better for painting delicate details.

Flat brushes can be used to paint wide marks.

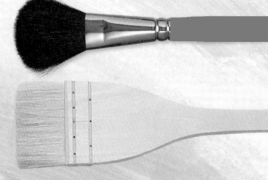

Wash brushes are usually large and soft, and can be used to create watercolor "washes"—large areas of blended color.

Thin brushes called riggers or liners are useful for painting detailed parts of an artwork.

FRIDA KAHLO
Mexican painter • 1907—1954

Frida Kahlo became used to spending a lot of time lying down as a child, after she caught polio at the age of six and was bedbound until she recovered.

Years later, at the age of eighteen, she was injured in a bus crash. While recovering, she was bored, so she decided to paint—and discovered that she loved it.

She sought out the Mexican artist Diego Rivera to ask for his advice about becoming an artist. They fell in love, and married. However, Diego often spent time away from her, and Frida was sad that she could not have children. Much of Frida's art shows the pain this caused her, as well as her ongoing physical pain due to the accident.

Self portraits
Frida is famous for her self-portraits. These paintings often emphasized her facial hair, and included plants and animals, such as monkeys, parrots, birds, and cats.

When Frida married Diego, she began wearing long skirts and fringed clothing in traditional Mexican styles.

A colorful life

Proud of her Mexican heritage, Frida wore traditional Mexican outfits, bold jewelry, and flowers in her hair. Her clothing and art were also inspired by colorful and symbolic Mexican art. She even painted her house in Mexico City a bright, cobalt blue—leading to it being known as *La Casa Azul* (The Blue House).

Over her life, Frida created 143 paintings, including fifty-five self-portraits. Because her paintings show her emotions and thoughts, her work was often called Surrealist. However, Surrealist art is about the unconscious mind, whereas Frida said she was not painting dreams, but real life.

Illness

Frida went through thirty operations throughout her life to help her recover from the bus crash. Bedbound after each operation, she painted on a special easel, and used a mirror on the ceiling to create self-portraits.

Diego Rivera is famous for murals (wall paintings) of historical Mexican events. He was much bigger than Frida, and the couple was nicknamed "the elephant and the dove."

Frida believed in communism—the idea that wealth and property should be shared by everyone equally. She included the communist thinker Karl Marx (shown above) in several paintings.

AMRITA SHER-GIL

Hungarian–Indian painter
1913—1941

Aged just 19, Amrita Sher-Gil won a gold medal in Paris, France, for one of her paintings, and she later became known as one of the creators of modern Indian art.

Amrita's mother was Hungarian and her father was Indian. She was born in Budapest, Hungary, but when Amrita was nine, she and her family moved to northern India. There, she learned to draw and paint. Later, Amrita studied art in Italy and France, but she decided to return to India where she became inspired by classical Indian art.

"I can only paint in India. Europe belongs to Picasso, Matisse, Braque... India belongs only to me."

Amrita was taught art by a private tutor from the age of eight. Amrita liked to paint people and used the staff in her house as models.

Painting in Paris

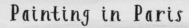

Amrita went to Paris when she was 16. Her early work, such as this self-portrait, was inspired by French Postimpressionist painters, such as Gauguin and Cézanne.

Painting everyday lives

Amrita wanted to show the real lives and emotions of poor people in India. She particularly liked painting women in their homes. While traveling around the country, she began to develop her own unique style. Her work became less realistic and used intense colors, including reds, golds, blues, and greens.

Tragically, when she was 28, and just before her first big exhibition was due to begin, Amrita became seriously ill and died. However, she left behind many paintings, and although she was not famous during her lifetime, she is now a celebrated artist.

Amrita's work was greatly influenced by miniature paintings made during the Mughal Empire in India. This style of painting showed life realistically, in bright colors.

Finding her style

Amrita's later painting style blended what she had learned in Europe and India. She created her 1935 painting *Three Girls* soon after her return to India.

CHARLOTTE SALOMON

German–Jewish painter
1917—1943

Living at a time when Jewish people were being murdered by the German government, Charlotte Salomon used art to record her short life. She produced hundreds of paintings showing personal and political events, which give us snapshots of history as well as her own story.

Charlotte came from a wealthy Jewish family in Berlin. She was sixteen when the anti-Jewish Nazis became Germany's ruling party. Life continued almost as normal for a while, and Charlotte started art school. But the Nazis began to stop Jews from doing everyday things, including studying, and violence against Jews increased.

A tragic start

When Charlotte was a child her mother tragically died. One of the *Life? or Theatre?* paintings shows Charlotte's mother telling her what heaven is like—a place where Jewish people believe they will go when they die.

We can guess about the times Charlotte was happiest from some of her paintings. In one, she sits on a calm-looking beach, holding a brush and paper in her hand.

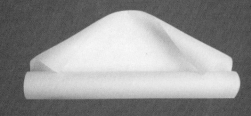

Almost half of the paintings in Life? or Theatre? *are covered with tracing paper, called overlays. On top, Charlotte wrote about what was happening in the painting, or what she was thinking or feeling.*

Living through art

Many of Charlotte's artworks show her painting, so we know this was an important part of her life. She wanted to show the good and bad parts of living.

Smashed glass

On the night of November 9, 1938, the Nazis attacked Jewish people and their property. The night became known as *Kristallnacht* (Crystal Night) because of all of the broken glass on the streets from smashed windows. Charlotte painted this in the artwork above.

Her life in pictures

Charlotte fled Germany to stay with her grandparents in France. But her troubles followed her, since she and her grandfather were imprisoned by the Nazis, who were occupying the country. They were freed after a short time, and she married another German-Jewish refugee.

Over the next two years, Charlotte painted herself and her loved ones, adding words, musical notes, and tracing paper on which she wrote words. She called the series *"Life? or Theatre?"* In 1943, she gave her art to a friend to keep safe. Soon after, she was captured and sent to a Nazi camp. Charlotte was killed just after she arrived, along with the baby she was expecting.

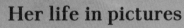

Like many Jewish people, Charlotte and her husband were killed at Auschwitz in Poland. Auschwitz was a concentration camp, set up by the Nazis to murder millions of Jews.

When Charlotte left Life? or Theatre? with a friend, she said, "Keep this safe, it is my whole life."

BETYE SAAR
American assemblage artist
1926—present

As a child, Betye was influenced by the Watts Towers in Los Angeles. These took 33 years to build out of cement and found objects such as shells, old tools, and broken glass.

Betye Saar's childhood love of **collecting odd things** turned into a skill for making art from found objects. Her enchanting works of art became part of America's first Black women's art exhibition. While Betye was growing up in Los Angeles, California, she often saw her mother using odds and ends to make things. Betye soon began to collect discarded bits and pieces for herself—such as bottle caps, feathers, and buttons. She made them into dolls and puppets, which were inspired by the fairy tales she loved reading. Betye enjoyed making things so much that she decided to study art at university.

Betye used many of the things she found as a child to make handicrafts from a craft book.

Finding her style

In 1967, Betye saw an exhibition by Joseph Cornell, who created boxes filled with various objects that Betye thought looked "jewel-like." She began creating her own boxes and wooden frames with objects that, together, told a story.

While still a student, Betye married the artist Richard Saar and had three daughters. Looking after the girls left little time for art, but Betye persevered. She took her daughters to lessons with her, and found the time to travel to countries in Africa and Central America to find objects and images to use in her art. Betye's art showed how Black people, and women in particular, are often not treated well. However, many of her artworks are meant to make people smile, too.

In 1970, Betye co-organized the first Black women's art exhibition in the United States, in her home city.

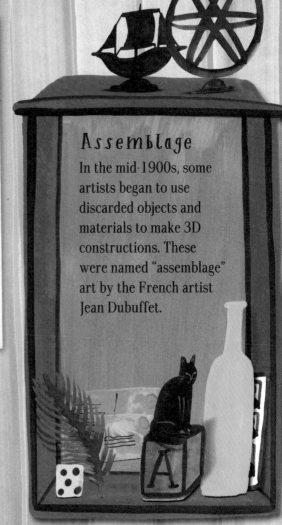

Assemblage

In the mid-1900s, some artists began to use discarded objects and materials to make 3D constructions. These were named "assemblage" art by the French artist Jean Dubuffet.

I wanted to get through to something new—a kind of painting that was my own.

The word "blackbird" was once used in a racist way, but in the 1960s it began to take on a new meaning. Betye explored this in her work "Blackbird," shown below.

113

ANDY WARHOL
American artist • 1928—1987

The youngest of three brothers, Andy Warhol was a shy boy who grew up in Pennsylvania. He was often ill, so he missed a lot of school. Instead, he stayed at home with his mother, drawing and coloring. When he was at school, Andy worked hard, especially at art until he was good enough to win a scholarship for drawing classes at university. After learning all he could from this course, he went on to a second university to study design.

In 1949, Andy moved to New York City to get a job in which he could use his creative talents. He became a successful illustrator, drawing pictures for magazines and advertisements. In 1961, he displayed his own paintings in a New York department store for the first time, and decided to work on his art full time.

From 1962, Andy produced silkscreen prints. These are made using stencils to add paint or ink to paper.

Andy famously made art showing cans of soup.

Pop art

Andy was among the first artists in America to work in Pop art. Artists used popular magazines, comics, celebrities, and products in their art for everyone to enjoy.

For a while, Andy carried a portable recorder with him wherever he went, recording what his friends said. When he died, he left many hours of recordings.

Tinfoil was used to decorate the walls of Andy's studio, The Factory.

Soup and screen prints

Andy made art featuring everyday images that viewers recognized. This was part of a new type of art, called Pop art. He showed the same food items over and again, and made pictures of famous people, repeating the same portrait in bright colors.

Andy's early works were paintings, but he found that printing methods meant he could produce more art faster. He worked during the day at his studio, then went to parties. He became famous, and many people called him "the father of Pop art."

Even as he became a famous artist, Andy continued to feel shy. He hid beneath wigs and sunglasses.

People who became known for going to parties with Andy and starring in his films, such as Edie Sedgwick, were called his "Superstars."

The Factory

In 1964, Andy opened a huge studio that became nicknamed "The Factory." Famous people constantly visited, parties were held, and Andy and his assistants made art there.

In the 1980s, Andy created two TV shows, Andy Warhol's TV and Andy Warhol's Fifteen Minutes. He also appeared on other TV programs.

115

Racism

Many artists have used art to challenge racism, which is the ill treatment of people because of their skin color or the country they are from. When a Black man named George Floyd was killed by a police officer in the United States, many murals were made to protest.

War

The violence of war has often caused artists to create powerful art. These artworks usually show the artist's own feelings about the fighting, for example by avoiding bright colors and painting lonely figures or sad scenes showing injured soldiers.

Feminism

The fight for women to be treated the same way as men, for example for them to earn the same pay at work, is called feminism. Artists using art to help this cause have often questioned how women are expected to behave. This might be by showing women in clothing they would not often be seen wearing.

Symbols are pictures that have a special meaning. They often appear in activist art. For example, a raised fist is used by the Black Lives Matter movement to show support for their cause.

ACTIVIST ART

Art isn't just there to look nice! Artists often make art as a way to help bring about changes in the world around them, for example if they see that people are being treated badly. This type of art is often bold, with shocking images or bright colors, to grab a viewer's attention. Once they've taken notice, viewers will hopefully go away and take action.

CLEAN SEAS

SAVE BEES

PROTECT TREES

Activist art doesn't just sit in galleries—many people make their own signs using pictures and stylish lettering to hold up at protests. These signs usually include symbols and slogans, which are phrases that stick in peoples' minds, often because they rhyme.

THERE IS NO PLANET B

The environment

Some artists use their art to protest against climate change, pollution, waste, or other issues that affect the environment. They might use nature, waste, or other elements from the world in their art.

Gender

In the past, most people thought that men and women should behave a certain way because of their gender. Now, many people, including some artists, question these ideas. The graffiti above uses symbols for both girls (left) and boys (right).

Powerful people

Art can help to inspire viewers to question people in power, or to support new governments. In the 1930s, many artists used their art to speak out against the German leader, Adolf Hitler, who ordered the deaths of millions of people.

YAYOI KUSAMA
Japanese artist • 1929—present

Often called the "princess of polka dots," Japanese artist Yayoi Kusama makes a lot of different types of art, with much of it covered in hundreds and sometimes thousands of dots! Her spotted creations include paintings, sculptures, performances, and installations.

When she was a child, Yayoi had a vision that scared her. She hallucinated that she was in a field of talking flowers. Because there were so many flowers, they all looked like dots and she felt as if she were disappearing into them. This strange experience has affected her ever since.

Yayoi's art is part of her everyday life. Yayoi wears dots, as often seen in her art, all over her clothes.

Yayoi was born and grew up in Japan. At twenty-nine, she moved to New York City, where she became known for her performance art, such as painting herself with dots.

The hallucination that Yayoi had when she was a little girl about being in the field of flowers has stayed with her throughout her life.

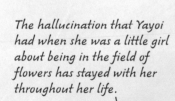

> "Our Earth is only one polka dot among a million stars in the cosmos. Polka dots are a way to infinity."

Popular exhibitions

In the 1960s, Yayoi began creating installations called "infinity mirror rooms"—mirrored rooms that she filled with dotted objects or hundreds of lights. The items or lights in the rooms reflect endlessly in the mirrors, which makes the viewer lose their sense of space. People loved Yayoi's dotted installations so much that in 2014, more people visited her *Infinite Obsession* exhibition than any other exhibition in the world.

Yayoi moved back to Japan in 1973 and today continues to create art and to write. In 2017, she opened a museum filled with her work in Japan's capital city, Tokyo.

Pumpkin, Central Harbourfront, Hong Kong, installed in 2018

Sculpture

Along with her installations, Yayoi creates sculptures made of all sorts of materials. Many of her sculptures are of giant, yellow pumpkins covered in black spots.

Yayoi has used pumpkins in her work since she was a child. To Yayoi, pumpkins can even represent an unusual kind of self-portrait.

Infinity mirror rooms

In Yayoi's mirror rooms the tiny lights seem to go on forever. The aim is for the viewer to feel as if they are part of something huge.

Infinity Mirrored Room, Gleaming Lights of the Souls, 2008

119

Marisol did her own thing from a young age—even changing her name from Maria Sol Escobar to "Marisol," by joining her first two names. She grew up to use art to question the ways that women are told to look and act.

Marisol showed early talent for art, and often won prizes for her drawing. Her art became a comfort to her after her mother died when Marisol was just eleven years old. Sent away by her father to boarding school in New York, Marisol drew to help calm her deep sadness. After finishing school, she chose to study art in Los Angeles, then in Paris, France, and finally back in New York.

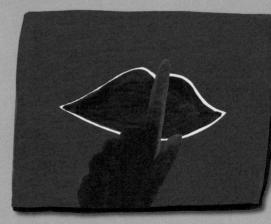

Marisol was greatly affected by her mother's death. She stopped speaking and often walked on her knees, which made them bleed. At school, she only spoke if she needed to ask or answer questions.

Feminist ideas

Marisol's wooden figures show the outfits women and girls were expected to wear. She also showed the things women were expected to do—such as take care of children.

MARISOL
Venezuelan–American sculptor
1930—2016

Wooden women

Marisol began making art that reflected life around her. She was inspired by folk art, which is usually handmade using skills passed down within communities. She also took ideas from art movements such as Surrealism, which explores dreams and the unconscious, or unawake, mind.

Marisol became most well-known for a series of flat, wooden figures with painted, realistic faces. Onto them she glued drawings, photographs, and pieces of clothing. The figures often reflected things that were happening in society, and Marisol was especially interested in the ways that people thought women should look and behave. She hoped that viewers of her art might notice how women were treated, too—and to wonder if it was fair.

Pop artist?

When Marisol was working, the Pop art movement was taking place. Pop artists, such as Andy Warhol (shown here with Marisol), made bright art, showing their thoughts about the world, so Marisol is often described as a Pop artist, too.

Good art is very peculiar. It's a mystery.

Marisol made many wooden sculptures of celebrities—including the President of France, Charles de Gaulle.

121

NAM JUNE PAIK

Korean–American video artist
1932—2006

Nam June Paik first trained as a pianist, but ended up creating a whole new type of art—video art. As a child, Nam escaped the Korean War with his parents and four older brothers and sisters, eventually arriving in Japan. There, he went to the University of Tokyo to study music. When he was twenty-four, he moved to West Germany and met music composers and artists who gave him new ideas about performance art. In his first exhibition, he placed televisions around a gallery and used magnets to warp the pictures on screen.

Without electricity there can be no art.

Nam was influenced by the experimental composer John Cage, who used noises from life in his work. One of Cage's most famous works of art has no sound at all.

When he was thirty, Nam joined a group of artists known as Fluxus. It contained painters, composers, designers, and poets, who performed their works rather than showing their artwork.

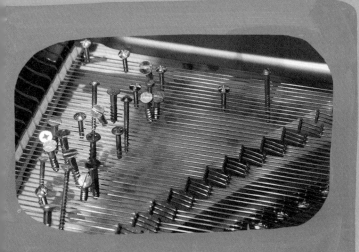

Nam was inspired to use new sounds. In some of his artworks he put objects inside pianos so they made odd noises when played.

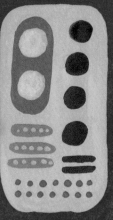

Video art

Often called "the father of video art," Nam began creating his art in the 1960s when television was first becoming in popular. Many other artists have worked with video since.

Mixing his interests

Nam was fascinated with radio and television, which were growing in popularity when he was young. In his career, he mixed all his interests together—art, music, and technology—creating sculptures with screens, live recordings, and unusual instruments. In 1964, he moved to New York where he met the cellist Charlotte Moorman, and they began working together. In their work "Robot Opera," a robot made by Nam said recordings of words while Charlotte played. Nam even imagined a day when the world would be connected by an "electronic super highway," and today we have just that—the internet.

Robots

Nam became known for making robots. At first, these were created with just wire and metal, but later, he used parts from radio and television sets.

ESTHER MAHLANGU

South African painter
1935—present

The houses of Ndebele communities in South Africa are traditionally painted inside and outside with large patterns made up of geometric shapes in bright colors. Growing up around these live-in artworks, Esther Mahlangu would eventually show the Ndebele tradition to the world.

Born on a farm in South Africa, Esther was taught the Ndebele practice of wall painting by her mother and grandmother. Using natural pigments (colors) mixed with cow dung and bright acrylic paints, Esther learned to create eye-catching patterns outlined in thick black lines. In 1986, French researchers saw her house paintings and invited her to create murals for an exhibition of international art in Paris, France, named *Magiciens de la terre* ("Magicians of the World").

Ndebele culture

The Ndebele are a group of people with a distinctive style of brightly colored art. As well as houses, they create colorful beadwork such as necklaces and headbands.

Ndebele designs are symmetrical, which means each half is a mirror image of the other. They also have straight edges, all drawn and painted by hand, without rulers.

Exhibiting and experimenting

Esther flew to France to take part in the exhibition, where thousands of people admired a house she painted in the vibrant Ndebele style, as well as murals that were soon shown across Europe and in South Africa. Mixing and creating original colors and patterns, she even became the first person to paint canvases in the Ndebele style.

To keep the tradition going, Esther started an art school in her own backyard. There, she teaches a new generation of young artists how to mix colors and paint straight lines and geometric patterns, building up their own Ndebele designs.

Rather than paintbrushes, Esther often uses chicken feathers to paint, in the Ndebele tradition.

Esther's designs have been sent into the sky on the tails of airplanes. On the ground, her art has been used to create eye-catching cars.

When looking at a Ndebele painting or mural, people get a smile of amazement on their faces.

Geometric patterns

Ndebele artists use repeat patterns of shapes such as diamonds and chevrons. They draw black outlines first, then fill these in with flat (unshaded), vivid colors.

DORIS SALCEDO
Colombian visual artist and sculptor
1958—present

Ordinary household items form the basis of much of Doris Salcedo's work, such as chairs and tables. These things often link to people who are missing from a family home, and Doris explores many other upsetting events in people's lives.

Doris grew up in Bogotá, the capital of Colombia, soon after the end of a war in the country between groups that wanted to form the government. However, fighting continued after the war ended—it is believed that clashes between the government and armed groups have caused the deaths of 200,000 people in Colombia during Doris's life so far. So, after studying art in Bogotá and New York City, Doris chose to make the effects of war and violence the main topic of her work.

Shibboleth

A large crack once snaked its way along the concrete floor of the Tate Modern in London, England. Doris created the crack, named Shibboleth, to remind people of country borders, and of refugees shunned in their new homes.

Doris has used chairs in several projects. In one, she lowered hundreds of them from a building in Bogotá. There, an historic clash between government soldiers and an armed group had led to around one hundred deaths.

A voice for victims

Doris wanted to show the grief of people left behind when family members or friends were killed. She spoke to children who had lost their parents, and tried to show the effect this had on their lives through her art. Her work slowly grew in popularity and in scale—her installations (artworks installed somewhere) grew from room-sized, within galleries, to public art that spanned the faces and heights of buildings.

With her art often in visible places around cities, Doris uses her installations to show everyone the horrors of the past and present, and the ways governments and individuals can cause suffering.

Doris's work often takes a lot of effort, to reflect how hard people work in her home country. She once sewed together thousands of rose petals into a cloth, in memory of a nurse who was kidnapped and murdered.

Politics

Doris's art has challenged governments both in her home country, over the ongoing fighting between the army and other groups, and abroad. Her art about refugees questions the actions of governments to help displaced people feel welcome.

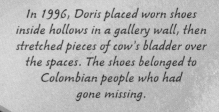

In 1996, Doris placed worn shoes inside hollows in a gallery wall, then stretched pieces of cow's bladder over the spaces. The shoes belonged to Colombian people who had gone missing.

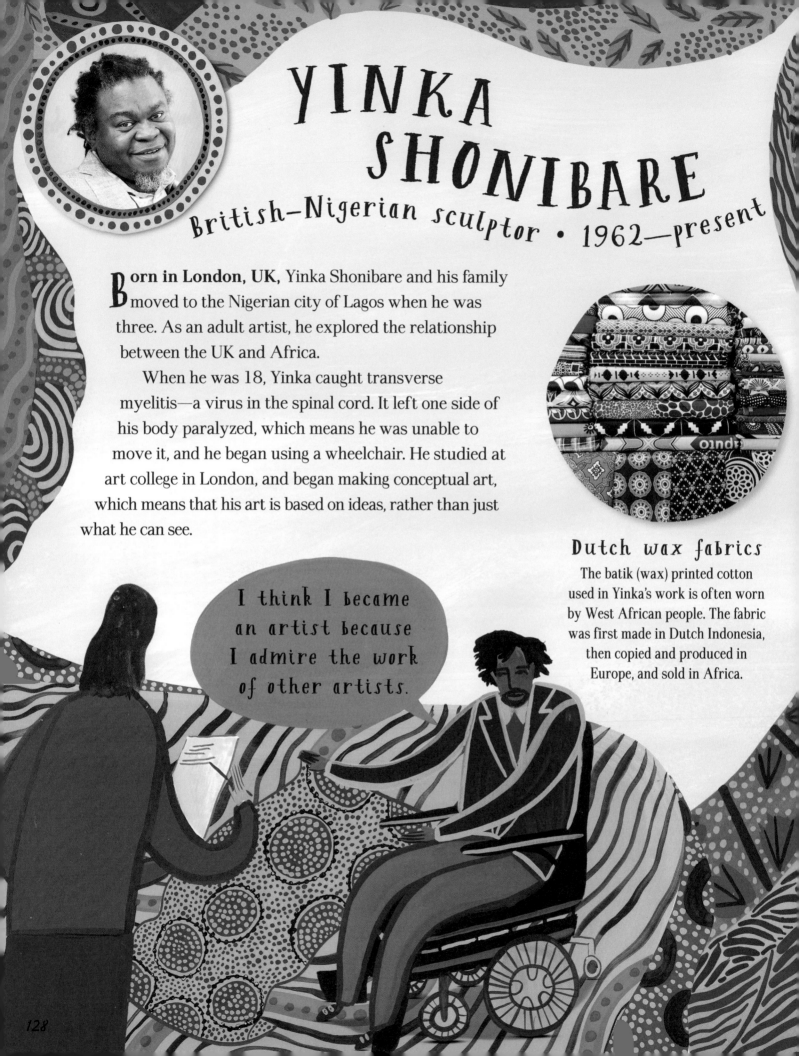

YINKA SHONIBARE

British-Nigerian sculptor • 1962—present

Born in London, UK, Yinka Shonibare and his family moved to the Nigerian city of Lagos when he was three. As an adult artist, he explored the relationship between the UK and Africa.

When he was 18, Yinka caught transverse myelitis—a virus in the spinal cord. It left one side of his body paralyzed, which means he was unable to move it, and he began using a wheelchair. He studied at art college in London, and began making conceptual art, which means that his art is based on ideas, rather than just what he can see.

Dutch wax fabrics

The batik (wax) printed cotton used in Yinka's work is often worn by West African people. The fabric was first made in Dutch Indonesia, then copied and produced in Europe, and sold in Africa.

> I think I became an artist because I admire the work of other artists.

128

Figures and fame

Yinka became a full-time artist a few years after leaving art college. Through his art, he explores subjects such as race and nationality, and how we feel about ourselves and others. Some of his best-known artworks are sculptures of figures dressed in vividly colored batik fabric. This material is made, sold, and bought in different countries—showing that nationality can often be a complicated topic.

He produces paintings, sculpture, photography, films, and installations, which is when art is built into a room. Yinka's art is popular, and it has been displayed in public places for many to see. He has been nominated for the Turner Prize—one of the most important art prizes in the world.

Yinka criticizes art of the past that only showed rich white people, such as the 18th-century painting above, by British artist William Hogarth. Yinka recreated Hogarth's art with Black figures.

Yinka's figures often have no head or strange objects instead of a head.

End of Empire

Yinka created End of Empire in England in 2016. By using globes in place of heads, he took away the figures' identities. This might show what empires did to the countries they controlled.

The Fourth Plinth

At each corner of London's Trafalgar Square is a plinth for a statue. One plinth stands empty, and when the council asked artists to fill it, Yinka created *Nelson's Ship in a Bottle*. As with all Yinka's art, it means something different to everyone.

JEAN-MICHEL BASQUIAT

American street artist • 1960—1988

Graffiti is often produced with a lot of skill, but not many people saw it as a form of art when Jean-Michel Basquiat was growing up. His graffiti-style art was an exciting addition to art galleries, where graffiti wasn't usually seen.

Jean-Michel's mother took him to museums as a boy in New York City, and encouraged him to draw. When he was eight years old, he was hit by a car and he had an operation to remove his spleen—a small organ under the ribs. While he recovered, Jean-Michel looked at a book called *Gray's Anatomy*, which showed how human bodies are structured. Using the book and his comics as inspiration, Jean-Michel began drawing figures.

> I don't listen to what art critics say. I don't know anybody who needs a critic to find out what art is.

Master of mixing

Jean-Michel's paintings mix ideas about graffiti, music, and sports, as well as African, Caribbean, Aztec, and Hispanic art. He used oil and acrylic paint, charcoal, oil pastels, and markers.

Graffiti art

Pictures, symbols, and words spray-painted, scribbled, or scratched onto walls are called graffiti. Jean-Michel often mimicked the style of graffiti in his canvas art.

Jean-Michel tackled important topics, such as racism. He saw that Black men were treated as less important in America, so he often used a crown to show their importance.

In 1979, Jean-Michel met the Pop artist Andy Warhol and they became good friends. In 1985, however, they fell out over their joint art exhibition and never made up.

From graffiti to gallery

As a teenager, Jean-Michel began spray-painting graffiti on walls with his friend, Al Diaz. He invented an imaginary character who preached about a pretend religion around New York City.

When Jean-Michel was twenty, people began to notice his graffiti, and he was invited to show some paintings at an exhibition called The Times Square Show. Suddenly, he became famous. Jean-Michel's work was exhibited at major art galleries around the world. His art was unlike anything the gallery visitors had seen before. They included scribbling and bold colors, and blended different types of art, such as graffiti, abstract expressionism, and cartoons. However, these styles were not learned at art school. Jean-Michel chose not to train with teachers. Instead, he said he learned about art by looking at it.

BANKSY
British street artist
Unknown—present

> Art should comfort the disturbed and disturb the comfortable.

One of the most famous artists working today has kept his identity a secret! Using the nickname Banksy and working in the dead of night, this artist has created artworks in public places all over the world.

Thought to be a man, Banksy started creating public art in the early 1990s. He spray-painted images on walls and trains in Bristol, UK, where there was already plenty of colorful street art and graffiti. By the 2000s, his unique style could be recognized—and spotted—all over the world. His artworks are often created with stencils, and mix humor with serious subjects, such as war.

Stencils allow Banksy to paint quickly. Early on in his career, he was influenced by a French graffiti artist, Blek le Rat, who is often called "the father of stencil graffiti."

A lot of people have tried to find out or guess Bansky's identity. Many people think he is a man named Robin Gunningham, but this has not been proven.

Banksy played soccer with the Easton Cowboys— a small UK team.

132

NEWS

Rats and royals

As well as creating art about important issues, Banksy has also used the money made from his artworks to support social causes. During the coronavirus pandemic in 2020, he painted a black-and-white picture of a boy playing with a nurse doll styled as a superhero, to recognize the bravery of doctors and nurses working at that time.

A year later, the artwork sold at auction for more than $23 million (£16 million), and he gave all the money to the UK's National Health Service (NHS).

Banksy often paints rats, apes, police officers, members of the royal family, and children—so if you see images of these out and about, take a closer look. It might just be a genuine Banksy.

Shredded art

In 2018, Banksy's painting *Balloon Girl* was offered for sale at an auction. Just after it was sold, it began moving down through the frame and passed through a hidden shredder that Banksy had put there secretly. The painting stopped halfway through the shredder.

INK-CREDIBLE NEW ARTWORK

This graffiti image from 2005 shows a figure posing as though he is about to violently throw a rock, but with flowers in his hand. This could be a way of showing that peace is better than war.

In 2015, in the UK seaside resort of Weston-super-Mare, Banksy built his own dark version of Disneyland. He called it Dismaland. Prepared in secret, it had ten new works by Banksy, and art from fifty-eight other artists.

TIMELINE

The history of art begins with the earliest creations we know about—made by artists tens of thousands of years ago. Since then, artists have been making works of art in many different formats and styles, about many different things.

Byzantine miniatures

Art in the Byzantine empire was mostly created to celebrate the Christian religion. Painted scenes, called miniatures, were made for Bibles.

The ancient Greeks began making sculptures of figures, showing what they thought to be perfect, beautiful features.

Made of brass and bronze, Benin bronzes are sculptures that were created for the royal court of the Oba (king).

`c.600 CE`

`c.600 CE`

`c.500 BCE`

`c.1180`

Porcelain was first invented in China, where painted, glossy ceramics were the most advanced in the world.

An especially creative period in European history, the Renaissance began in the 1300s and ended during the 1600s.

`c.1300`

Baroque painting

Made to support Catholicism, Baroque paintings usually show dramatic scenes and use rich colors that contrast.

Ukiyo-e became a popular type of art in Japan, featuring paintings and prints, on topics ranging from famous figures to natural scenes.

By the 19th century, modern cartoons had emerged as simplified, humorous drawings.

`c.1600`

`1670`

`1814`

Pop art

Starting in the 1950s, Pop artists created art out of aspects of the commercial world, such as celebrities, comics, and packaging.

Surrealists began exploring the subconscious (unawake) mind, which some thought was revealed through dreams.

`c.1950`

`c.1920`

Photorealists began creating images that looked photographically real, painted or drawn with precise details.

`c.1970`

Cave painting

Most cave paintings were made deep inside caves, where they would rarely be seen. Historians believe that these were created for special, religious purposes.

c.64,000 BCE

Mesopotamian civilizations in what is now West Asia made sculptures of people and animals, using materials such as stone and gold.

c.3100 BCE

Egyptian sculptures of gods and pharaohs were made from stone, and many were painted. Some were huge, reaching higher than two-story buildings.

c.3000 BCE

Lullubi rock reliefs

In Iran, ancient rock reliefs made by the Lullubi people show scenes such as a king with someone he has captured at his feet.

Celtic craftworkers—who lived in parts of northern Europe—produced intricate objects in bronze, copper, and gold.

c.1000 BCE

c.2300 BCE

The Indus Valley civilization in what is now Pakistan made sculptures, pottery, and ornaments, many of which showed figures.

c.2500 BCE

Photography

The invention of photography changed art dramatically. Images could now be captured exactly as they appeared in the real world, though many artists created their own made-up scenes.

A style of painting, called Impressionism, began in France. Artists painted rapidly, with visible brushstrokes and bright colors.

c.1865

Post-Impressionism

This highly influential art made between 1886 and 1905 was mainly by French artists who explored color, line, and emotion.

c.1885

c.1850

Cubism

In the early 1900s, artists in Europe began showing several viewpoints at once, as part of a movement called Cubism.

In Russia, artists began making abstract structures with industrial materials, believing that art should directly reflect the modern world.

1915

1907

Abstract art grew popular from 1900, which did not show anything from the world that we recognize. It often has underlying meanings.

c.1900

MORE ARTISTS

Guan Daosheng
1262–1319

Also known as Guan Zhongji or Lady Zhongji, the Chinese painter and poet Guan Daosheng lived and worked during the early Yuan Dynasty (1271–1368). She was an expert at calligraphy, and at painting on bamboo.

Sandro Botticelli
c.1445–1510

During his early career, the Italian painter Sandro Botticelli was famous for his elegant style, but he later became unfashionable and lost popularity. He painted many religious and mythological subjects, including his most famous works, *The Birth of Venus* and *Primavera*.

Leonardo da Vinci
1452–1519

The Italian genius Leonardo da Vinci was a painter, sculptor, architect, engineer, scientist, and inventor. His portrait the *Mona Lisa* became one of the most famous in the world, after it was stolen from an art gallery in 1911, creating a news story that was widely talked about.

Sofonisba Anguissola
c.1532–1625

The eldest in an Italian family of six daughters and a son, Sofonisba Anguissola became an internationally famous and sought-after painter, which was unusual for a woman at the time. She mainly painted portraits and images from Christianity.

Mary Cassatt
1844–1926

Although born in the US, Mary Cassatt lived in Paris, France from the age of thirty. Before settling there, she traveled to Italy, Spain, Belgium, and the Netherlands to study painting. She became involved with the Impressionist movement, and produced many paintings, pastels, and prints.

Henry Ossawa Tanner
1859–1937

Henry Ossawa Tanner was the first African American painter to achieve international fame. Although he was born in the US, he later moved to Paris, where he experienced less ill treatment because of his skin color than in the US. He was well known for his Christian scenes.

Käthe Kollwitz
1867–1945

German artist Käthe Kollwitz showed poor and suffering people, especially those who lived through war. Tragedies in her own life helped her to understand other people's feelings, and she experimented with printmaking techniques to try to capture her subjects' feelings.

Marcel Duchamp
1887–1968

The French artist Marcel Duchamp insisted that art should be about ideas—which was a new theory at the time. He avoided making art in the same way as those who had worked before, for example by inventing "readymades"—which meant using everyday objects as artworks. He became one of the first artists to make Conceptual art.

Judith Jans Leyster
1609–1660

Born in the Netherlands, Judith Leyster was one of the few professional women painters during a period known as the Dutch Golden Age. Influenced by Caravaggio, she painted many dramatically lit paintings of happy people playing music and drinking.

Élisabeth Louise Vigée Le Brun
1755–1842

In 1787, French artist Élisabeth Vigée Le Brun created a scandal when she painted herself showing her teeth! She also painted a portrait of queen Marie Antoinette, who was overthrown in the French Revolution. Élisabeth fled France for Italy because of this connection.

J. M. W. Turner
1775–1851

The English painter, printmaker, and watercolorist J. M. W. Turner helped to make landscape painting a popular form of art. His work had a distinct style that many people tried to copy, using a technique that suggests emotions, and painting light and weather in a unique way.

Claude Monet
1840–1926

One of the leading figures of Impressionism, the French artist Claude Monet painted nature as he saw it. He used short brush marks to quickly build up the effects of light, weather, and color, which allowed him to capture short moments in time.

Claude Cahun
1894–1954

In 1914, French Surrealist photographer, sculptor, and writer Lucy Schwob took the name Claude Cahun, as a sign of a neutral gender (neither a boy nor a girl). Claude created photographic self-portraits dressed as different characters, such as a doll and a body builder.

Eileen Agar
1899–1991

Argentinian-born Eileen Agar moved to London when she was twelve. She became a Surrealist painter and object-maker, inspired by her imagination and dreams. Many of her artworks were "assemblages"—made of several objects she had found.

Barbara Hepworth
1903–1975

The career of British sculptor Barbara Hepworth lasted more than fifty years. Her 3D, abstract forms explored the relationship between people and nature, as well as music and the landscape around her studio in St. Ives in Cornwall, UK.

Tove Jansson
1914–2001

Finnish writer, painter, and cartoonist Tove Jansson is mostly known for her Moomin books for children. She also created many more stories and novels for both children and adults, as well as book covers, cartoons, and paintings.

Joan Hill
1930–2020

Of Native American ancestry, Joan Hill descended from both Muscogee Creek and Cherokee chiefs. She painted with different styles and materials, often using Native American artistic techniques, and won many awards for her art.

Gerhard Richter
1932–present

German artist Gerhard Richter originally trained in painting realistically. However, he began blending his early style with abstract features, to show underlying meanings in his work. Inspired by several twentieth century art movements, he also works with photography.

Frank Bowling
1934–present

Born in Guyana, in the Caribbean, Frank Bowling moved to London, UK, when he was nineteen. He studied art there and became inspired by different art movements to mix realistic, symbolic, and abstract ideas in his work, creating his own distinct style.

Nasreen Mohamedi
1937–1990

Best known for her large, fine line abstract drawings, Nasreen Mohamedi became one of the most important Modernist Indian artists. Her large abstract works are usually made up of geometric lines that represent such things as energy and awareness.

Marina Abramović
1946–present

Avoiding traditional art and materials, Yugoslavian-born Marina Abramovic uses her own body as her work. Her performance art is usually dramatic as she often puts herself in danger, exploring themes such as trust and survival.

Cindy Sherman
1954–present

American artist Cindy Sherman is famous for taking photographs of herself dressed up. Her costumes and makeup in these photos question stereotypical ideas held about people, particularly older or younger women.

Grayson Perry
1960–present

English artist Grayson Perry produces ceramic vases, tapestries, and paintings. His vases are classically shaped and decorated in bright colors, showing elements of his own life. He is also well known for the clothes he wears, which include bright, eye-catching dresses.

Takashi Murakami
1962–present

Brightly colored artworks that draw on ideas from Japanese and Pop art have made Japanese artist Takashi Murakami famous around the world. Unlike most artists, he employs workers in factories to produce and sell his art.

David Hockney
1937–present

Draftsman, printmaker, stage designer, and photographer, David Hockney was involved with the Pop art movement in the 1950s. Born in the UK, his distinctive style includes bright colors, simplified shapes, and often huge paintings created on his iPad.

Hayao Miyazaki
1941–present

A Japanese animator, director, producer, screenwriter, author, and manga artist, Hayao Miyazaki is world famous for his animated feature films. They explore themes such as human relationships with nature, and have won some of the most prestigious international film awards.

Gloria Petyarre
1942–2021

The Aboriginal artist Gloria Petyarre became known for her batik painting style. Although she was based in Australia, she traveled around the world for her art. Mixing colors directly on her canvas, she used both bold and delicate brushstrokes, and vivid and natural colors.

Marta Minujín
1943–present

Marta Minujín studied art from an early age in her native Argentina. She began her career as a painter, but then started using unusual materials, inspired by everyday experiences such as viewing advertisements and listening to pop music.

Pipilotti Rist
1962–present

Known for her installations that combine visual art and sound, Swiss artist Pipilotti Rist creates whole art environments. She often transforms a space to allow her viewers to feel as if they are inside her work.

Lee Bul
1964–present

Working with several types of art, including performance, sculpture, painting, installation, and video, Lee Bul is most known for her strange sculptures and landscape paintings. She explores serious topics, such as how technology affects our world.

Olafur Eliasson
1967–present

Olafur Eliasson is an Icelandic-Danish artist who creates large installations and sculptures. Using elements such as light, water, and temperature, he creates entire art experiences, such as his 2003 installation, *The Weather Project*.

Amy Sherald
1973–present

American painter Amy Sherald mainly creates portraits of African American people, in ordinary situations. She often simplifies what she sees, using shades of gray for skin tones, to highlight people's reactions to skin color and race.

GLOSSARY

abstract art
Art that does not show objects or people in a lifelike way, but uses bold colors and shapes

apprentice
Young person sent to help and learn from an artist

architect
Person who designs buildings

art movement
Period of time when a group of artists produce work with similar themes or techniques

Baroque
Period in the 17th and 18th centuries when some art and architecture was grand and dramatic

bust
Statue of the head and shoulders

calligraphy
Writing where the letters or characters are drawn beautifully

canvas
Material stretched over a wooden frame on which paintings are drawn. Canvas fabric is often made from flax plants

contrast
Noticeable difference between two things, for example areas of light and dark in a painting

Cubism
Art movement of the 20th century in which the objects of paintings were shown from different angles and often made up of geometric shapes

depict
Show

depth
Sense of perspective in pictures

exhibition
Display of several artworks by one or many artists. Exhibitions are usually held in galleries

Expressionism
Art movement of the 20th century in which paintings tried to show emotions or a particular mood

figurative art
Art that is realistic

fine art
Art that is made purely to be looked at

folk art
Art usually made by people in their homes in small communities for practical purposes

fresco
Wall painting made directly on wet plaster

Futurism
Art movement of the 20th century in which "the future" featured as a subject, such as in technology

geometric
Made from recognizable shapes, such as squares and triangles, or bold lines

Impressionism
Art movement of the 19th century in which paintings were created quickly, often outdoors, to capture an "impression" of the subject, not focusing on details

installation
Three-dimensional artwork that is set up, or installed, in a space

mineral

Inorganic substances, not of plant or animal origin. Some minerals are crushed to make pigments

miniature

Very small painting

modern art

Some art that was made from the late 19th century to the late 20th century, by artists who tried out various new ideas and methods

mosaic

Artwork made by gluing many tiny tiles next to each other to create an image

motif

Design or symbol that is repeated throughout a pattern or an artist's work

perspective

Sense of depth in a picture created by making more distant objects smaller

pigment

Colorful substance used to make paints. Pigments can be made from plants, minerals, and rocks, or be created in labs

Pointillism

Art movement in the 19th century in which paintings were created by dotting thousands of spots near each other

Pop art

20th century art movement in which ordinary objects are often shown, sometimes in collages or in colorful comic-book-style

portrait

Picture of a person. Portraits may be of a full body or only of a person's head

print

Artwork made by pressing an object onto a surface and leaving a mark

Realism

Art movement of the 19th century in which everyday activities were shown, painted in a lifelike way

Renaissance

Period from the 14th to the 17th centuries when new ideas in art and science spread throughout Europe and beyond, inspired by classical Greece

sculpture

Three-dimensional artwork. Sculptures can be carved out of wood or stone, or be built from clay, metal, or other materials

self-portrait

Picture of an artist created by themselves

shade

Darkness of a color, or darker areas in paintings that make an object or person look three-dimensional

sketch

Quick drawing, usually in pencil, that can be a study or plan for a later artwork

still life

Artwork created by drawing the objects in front of you, often collected together on a table

study

Test drawing of a particular object, which may be used as practice for a future artwork

stylized

Illustration in a particular style that doesn't try to make the subject look real

subject

Particular object, person, or landscape shown in a painting

tapestry

Artwork made by sewing images onto a large piece of fabric

tempera

Type of paint made from dry pigments added to a wet glue, such as egg yolk, which makes it liquid

tone

Brightness or darkness of a color

INDEX

ACKNOWLEDGEMENTS

About the author

Susie Hodge MA, FRSA, is an art historian, author artist and journalist. She has written over 160 books for both adults and children – and several for DK. She also sometimes appears on radio and TV, writes magazine articles, and material for museums and galleries, and she runs workshops and gives talks and lectures around the world. In her office, she is often joined by her three cats, Albert, Stanley and Princess.

This book is for my own works of art – Katie, Jonathan and Max.

About the illustrator

Jessamy Hawke has been drawing since she was old enough to hold a pencil. She lives between London and Dorset, in the UK, where she enjoys walking along the coast and finding spots to sit and paint outdoors. Jessamy also illustrated *Explorers, Inventors* and *Scientists*, other DK children's books. When she's in the studio, she's kept company by her dog, Mortimer, and her two cats, Marcel and Rhubarb.

To my wonderful mum Jenny, and my late grandfather Eddie, the two artists who first inspired me to paint, and have brought such colour to our lives.

About the consultant

Dr Stephen Haddelsey is a British historian and the author of seven books; he has also edited three historical manuscripts for their first publication. He is a Fellow of both the Royal Geographical Society and the Royal Historical Society, and an Honorary Research Fellow at the University of East Anglia.

DK would like to thank: Yilin Wang, Sukyeon Cho, Nozomi Uematsu, Ana Elena Gonzalez Trevino, and Dee Hudson for additional consulting; Syed Md Farhan and Roohi Rais for cut-outs; Steve Crozier for repro work; Polly Goodman and Laura Gilbert for proofreading; and Helen Peters for the index